LEWIS

INTERNATIONAL, INC.

The Author

Dr Armen Victorian is a researcher and writer who lives in England. He has been conducting research into mind control, intelligence, and other related topics for many years. He is currently campaigning with the Red Cross and various human rights organisations to curb use of the latest range of weapons, and to prevent even further damage and suffering.

First published in Great Britain in 1999 by VISION Paperbacks, a division
of Satin Publications Limited.
This edition is published in the United States in 2000 by Lewis
International, Inc.

Lewis International Inc.
2201 NW 102nd Place # 1
Miami, Fl 33172
USA
Tel: 305 436 7984 / 800 259 5962
Fax: 305 436 7985 / 800 664 5095

Cover Image: ©2000 Nickolai Globe
Layout: Justine Hounam
Printed and bound in Great Britain by Biddles Ltd.

©2000 Dr Armen Victorian
ISBN: 0-9666771-9-6

The Mind Controllers

Dr Armen Victorian

Acknowledgments

The author would like to thank Tom Gray, without whom this book would not have been possible; Robin Ramsay for his support, and the continued publication of articles in Lobster; and all at Vision Paperbacks for their hard work.

Contents

Dedication

I dedicate this book to those innocent victims who have suffered from physical or mental abuse and torture inflicted upon their minds and bodies by the state, whatever flag they fly under. I thank the courageous individuals for telling the world about their torment. And, I am grateful to those institutions that stood by their side and fought for their human rights – rights which are still violated by states under the protection of their national security acts. No amount of compensation is sufficient for raping or killing the mind.

Introduction

Intelligence is nothing new. It dates back as far as the Old Testament when God commanded Moses to send agents to 'spy out the land of Canaan'. It is also referred to in 400 BC by the Chinese military strategist Sun Tzu in his book, 'The Art of War', in which he emphasised the importance of good intelligence by noting that to 'win 100 battles is not the acme of skills. To find security without fighting is the acme of skill.'

It was used in the 13th Century by the Mongol leader Subotai in directing his forces to spectacular military successes in their invasion of Europe. Such use of intelligence was not mirrored in Europe until much later. As Allen Welsh Dulles, for nine years Director of Central Intelligence, states in 'The Craft of Intelligence', European rulers in the Middle Ages 'were not very well informed about the Byzantine Empire and the Eastern Slavs; they knew even less of the Moslem world; and they were almost completely ignorant of anything that went on in Central and East Asia.'

However, in 16th century England, Sir Francis Walsingham, principal State Secretary to Queen Elizabeth I, developed and sustained a network of dozens of intelligence agents dispersed to foreign lands. He recruited his people from Cambridge and Oxford, nurtured the art of espionage, and had the tools and techniques for making and breaking codes. Thus in a very real sense, aspects of the intelligence service established by Walsingham foreshadowed modern intelligence organisations.

According to The Central Intelligence Agency's Fact Book, the United States has carried on foreign intelligence activities since the days of George Washington, but only since World War Two have they been co-ordinated on a Government-wide basis. Even before Pearl Harbour, President Franklin D. Roosevelt was concerned about American intelligence deficiencies. He asked New York lawyer, William J. Donovan, to draft a plan for an intelligence service.

The Office of Strategic Services (OSS) was therefore established in June 1942 with a mandate to collect and analyse strategic information required by the Joint Chiefs of Staff, and to conduct special operations not assigned to other agencies. During the War it supplied policy makers with essential facts and intelligence estimates, and it often played an important role in directly aiding military campaigns. But the OSS never received complete jurisdiction over all foreign intelligence activities. Since the early 1930s the FBI had been responsible for intelligence work in Latin America, and the military services protected their areas of responsibility.

In October 1945, the OSS was disbanded and its function was absorbed by the State and War Departments. But the need for a post-war centralised intelligence system was clearly recognised. Eleven months earlier, Donovan, by then a Major General, had submitted to President Roosevelt a proposal calling for the separation of OSS from Joint Chiefs of Staff with the new organisation having direct Presidential supervision. Donovan proposed an 'organisation which will procure intelligence both by overt and covert methods and would at the same time provide intelligence guidance, determine national intelligence objectives, and correlate the intelligence material collected by all government agencies.'

Under Donovan's plan, a powerful centralised agency would have co-ordinated all the intelligence services. He also proposed that this agency should have authority to conduct 'subversive operations abroad', but with 'no police or law enforcement functions, either at home or abroad.' This plan drew heavy fire: the military services generally opposed a complete merger; the State Department thought it should supervise all peacetime operations affecting foreign relations; and, the FBI supported a system whereby military intelligence world-wide would be handled by the armed services and all civilian activities under its own jurisdiction.

In response to this policy debate, President Harry S. Truman established the Central Intelligence Group (CIG) in January 1946, directing it to co-ordinate existing departmental intelligence, supplementing but not supplanting their services. This was all to be done under the direction of the National Intelligence Agency (NIA) composed of a Presidential representative, and the Secretaries of State, War and Navy. Rear Admiral Sidney W. Souers, USNR, who was the Deputy Chief of Naval Intelligence, was appointed the first director of Central Intelligence.

As little as twenty months later, the NIA and its operating component, the CIG, were disestablished. and, under the provisions of the National Security Act of 1947 (which became effective on 18 September 1947) the National Security Council (NSC) and the Central Intelligence Agency (CIA) were established.

Most of this statute's specific assignments given to the CIA, as well as the prohibitions on police and internal security functions, closely follow both the original 1944 Donovan plan and the Presidential directives which created the CIG. The 1947 Act charged the CIA with co-ordinating the nation's intelligence activities, and correlating, evaluating and disseminating intelligence that affects national security. In addition, the Agency was to perform such other duties and functions relating to intelligence as the NSC might direct. The Act also made the DCI responsible for protecting intelligence sources and methods.

It was further stated that both the Director and Deputy Director of Central Intelligence were to be appointed by the President, subject to confirmation by the Senate. An amendment of 4 April 1953 authorised such appointments to be made either from individuals in civilian life, or from commissioned officers of the armed services (either in active or retired status), provided that 'at no time shall the two positions... be occupied simultaneously by commissioned officers.'

In 1949, the Central Intelligence Agency Act was passed supplementing the 1947 Act. Congress enacted additional provisions permitting the Agency to use confidential fiscal and administrative procedures, and exempting the CIA from many of the usual limitations on the expenditure of Federal funds. It provided that CIA funds could be included in the budgets of other departments, and then transferred to the Agency without regards to the restrictions placed on the initial appropriation. This Act is the statutory authority for the secretary of the Agency's budget.

In order to further protect intelligence sources and methods from disclosure, the 1949 Act exempted the CIA from having to disclose its 'organisational, functions, names, officials, titles, salaries, or number of personnel employed.' Under these acts of Congress, the Director serves as the principal advisor to the President and the NSC on all matters of foreign intelligence which relate to national security. The CIA's responsibilities are carried out subject to various directives and controls by the President and the NSC.

Today the CIA reports regularly to the Senate Select Committee on Intelligence (SSCI), and to the House Permanent Select Committee on Intelligence (HPSCI), as required by the Intelligence Oversight Act of 1980. The Agency also reports regularly to the Defense Subcommittees of the Appropriations Committees in both Houses of Congress. Moreover, the Agency also provides substantive briefings to the Senate Foreign Relations Committee, House Committee on Foreign Affairs, and the Armed Services Committees in both bodies as well as other Committees and individual members.

Executive Order 12333, issued by President Reagan on 4 December 1981, gives the DCI authority to develop and implement the National Foreign Intelligence Programme budget, and to co-ordinate the tasking of all intelligence community collection elements. In addition to staff elements of the Office of the DCI, the intelligence community in The United States consists of the Central Intelligence Agency; the National Security Agency; the Defence Intelligence Agency; the offices within the Department of Defense which are responsible for the collection of specialised national foreign intelligence through reconnaissance programs; the Bureau of Intelligence and Research of State; and the intelligence elements of the military services, the FBI, and the Department of Treasury and Energy.

For reasons that will become clear, an area which has been of great interest to those researching the methods and techniques of mind control is radiation. What follows shows not only that the CIA has been involved in the testing of radiation for mind control purposes, but that this experimentation has involved the unethical use of human 'guinea pigs'.

The CIA is not alone in exploring the use of mind control techniques but undoubtedly, along with the former Soviet Union, it is the leader in this area. Much of its work is of course classified and work farmed out to other institutions is equally shrouded in mystery. There is however, one way of penetrating this fascinating and worrying new area of research.

Diligent use of the Freedom of Information Act in the US helps to cast light on the advances that have been made in controlling the way people think and act – and how it is possible to sap their will to resist. The Act allows the most humble citizen to demand the disclosure of documents, although inevitably some will be heavily censored or not released at all.

That is how much of the information in this book has been pieced together. Where primary sources of information are withheld, the extent of mind control research and the development of non-lethal weapons can be discerned by delving into other files held by the US bureaucracy. They reveal not only what has been going on in the US, but also in the Eastern Bloc and in other Western countries.

Inevitably, however, it is an incomplete picture. What the mind controllers were and are doing may be only hinted at in the footnote to a memo or, unguardedly, in the memoirs of a retired researcher. This book is therefore a compilation of my investigations into these and many other sources, which are continuing. As it goes to press, I still have hundreds of outstanding Freedom of Information Act enquiries that await a response. Nevertheless there is more than enough here to show that sinister and secret new techniques are being exploited that alas are no longer in the realm of science fiction. We must all be aware of this threat so that those who would wish to take liberties with democracy, and with our freedom to think, are deterred.

Chapter One

The Secret Agenda

Immediately after the end of the Second World War, the Western allies identified the Soviet Union and Eastern Bloc countries as their new enemy. An entirely new kind of non-war began, a Cold War. With growing paranoia surrounding communism, fuelled by its 'Black Budget', the US renewed its interest in the subject of mind control.

The methods and technologies that were developed over the following five decades resulted in as much pain and suffering for the targets of these operations as during the 'real war' which had just ended. In most cases, the victims could not begin to understand the logic of their becoming a target in the silent global warfare between the emerging superpowers. Mostly, the victims were innocent people caught in the cross-fire. At other times people were used as guinea pigs in the experimental and development stages of the new science of mind control.

Almost five months after the CIA's creation in December 1947, the National Security Council held its first meeting. James Forrestal, the Secretary of Defense, pushed for the CIA to begin a 'secret war' against the Soviets. This was in response to the growing concern in America that communist agents had infiltrated all levels of society and needed to be flushed out and destroyed. It is interesting to note that by May 1949, Forrestal had become intensely paranoid about being surrounded, or followed, by communists. Whilst under treatment for a mental breakdown at the Bethesda Naval Hospital, he killed himself jumping out of an open window. Forrestal, in a sense, became the first victim of the growing paranoid, overkill policy adopted by the United States and which, in many ways, continues today.

The Mind Controllers

British policy up to this time had been somewhat different. Today in the Public Records Office, there are over 16,000 document files covering the development of psychological warfare up to 1948.

Forrestal's initiative at the 1947 meeting led to the issue of a secret order, NSC-4A, under the CIA's new director, Rear Admiral Roscoe Hillenkoetter. He was instructed to commence the execution of psychological warfare operations (psy-ops) in Europe. This involved answering a crucial question – did the CIA have a legal, not to mention moral, right to conduct such activities abroad? General Counsellor Lawrence Housten declared in a memorandum that the CIA had no legal jurisdiction as an intelligence agency. He added that it would also be illegal for the CIA to be used by the President as a 'secret army'.

Nonetheless, it was decided that the communist threat was an issue that took priority over constitutional rights. NSC-4A was therefore supplemented by a further instruction, NSC-10/2, to create a Presidential Secret Order which had the effect of greatly increasing the CIA's powers. As a result, the CIA formally established its covert action branch; the Office of Policy and Co-ordination (OPC).

The Agency immediately embarked on a wide range of research programmes and operations, the aim being to discover the best means of utilising psy-op techniques in combating the enemies of Western democracy. This work was not new and, as we shall see later, it was based on research dating back as far as 1923.

As a result of events during the Second World War, the concept of running a secret 'black' project was no longer novel for Western military and intelligence planners. Projects such as the Manhattan Project (the US secret atomic bomb programme) had given birth to an entirely new generation of operations and, because of them, a moral precedent had been established which made it much easier for psy-op programme champions to argue their case. The existence of all these operations – 'Black Projects' funded by 'Black Budgets' – were withheld not only from the public, but also from Congress for reasons of national security.

The basic concept for the first of these Black Projects was conceived, as far as we can tell, on 9 October 1941 – two months before the bombing of Pearl Harbour by the Japanese.

Vannevar Bush, the Dean of Engineering at Massachusetts Institute of Technology (MIT), explained to Franklin D. Roosevelt how a 25 pound atomic bomb could explode with the estimated power of 3.6 million pounds of dynamite, providing the means for the US to win the next war. Roosevelt decided, without consulting the representatives of the people in Congress, that the US should proceed immediately, in utmost secrecy, to develop such a weapon. He also decided to make the funds for the project available from 'a special source available for such an unusual purpose.'[1]

It was estimated at the time that the entire project would cost $100 million. This proved to be drastically wrong. Over the next four years $2.19 billion of American tax-payers money was spent. According to General Leslie R. Groves, the Commander of the Manhattan Project, such huge spending 'required unorthodox' and 'unusual procedures'.[2] The creation of such a system of funding provided the blueprint for other clandestine projects, some of which continue to this day.

Secrecy shrouded the Manhattan Project to the extent that Vice-President Harry Truman knew nothing about it. (In fact it remained so secret that it was several years before a President was allowed to see the military plans for using such a bomb.)

The two key figures involved were Franklin D. Roosevelt and Winston Churchill, who had secretly agreed between themselves in September 1944 that the bomb, 'might, perhaps, after mature consideration, be used against the Japanese.'[3]

Roosevelt died on 12 April 1945, and when Truman took office, the project remained top secret. The Secretary of War, Henry Stimpson, found a moment to murmur in Truman's ear that America had 'an enormous project to build a new explosive of almost unbelievable power.'

In later years Truman recalled Stimpson's words and commented: 'His statements left me puzzled.'[4] Such was the scale of secrecy surrounding the first American Black Project.

The Manhattan Project meant that by the time the newly created CIA obtained the go-ahead to establish its covert operations branch in Europe in 1947, the US Government had already gained vast experience in the initiation of secret operations conducted without the knowledge of Congress. Furthermore, now that the CIA was no longer just collecting foreign intelligence, it quickly evolved to become the President's secret army.

One of the main areas to be investigated by the CIA was mind or personality control. In fact, many other branches of the US Government took part in the study of this area, including the Atomic Energy Commission (Department of Energy), NASA, and various Department of Defense sub-units.

Under the protection of 'national security', these branches embarked on a wide range of macabre programmes, including assassination squads, brain washing programmes, civilian spying, drug trafficking, illegal arms sales, fomenting civil wars and toppling foreign governments.

Although not officially endorsed, each President in turn gave his approval for the continuance of such projects. While the CIA developed its science of psychological warfare techniques, it also expanded the programme to include such subjects as UFOs and Extra Sensory Perception (ESP).

The initial CIA mind control projects brought about encouraging results and it was decided they merited further investigation. General William 'Wild Bill' Donovan, director of the Office of Strategic Services (OSS), had already tasked his team – which included Drs Edward Strecker, Winfred Overshulser, George White and Harry J. Anslinger – to modify human behaviour and perception through chemical means.

Donovan's team was determined to create a 'truth serum' by experimenting with ego relief narcotics such as scopaline, barbiturates, peyote, marijuana, and mescaline. These efforts received an extra boost when a number of Nazi chemical specialists (brought into the US via the Operation Paperclip programme) began to work closely with the American secret services.

Scientists such as Karl Tauboek, whose efforts to create a 'truth serum' were crucial in the history of mind control, provided the CIA with a wealth of important information. Tauboek obtained his data from ruthless human experimentation. Frederick Hoffman, another Nazi researcher, discovered a paralysis-inducing conch shell venom. At the same time another group of Nazi scientists – Karl Rarh, Theodore Wagner-Jauregg and Hans Turit – continued their previous wartime covert research. They worked from American laboratories, developing poison and nerve gases such as tabun and sarin. They worked on these projects despite their active and known involvement in the Holocaust. A decision had obviously been taken determining that the military necessity to develop new mind control drugs and techniques outweighed any moral issues raised by the origination of the research data.

In 1977 Sidney Gottlieb, an important MKULTRA administrator, (MKULTRA will be discussed in more depth later) was taken before a Senate sub-hearing. He was there to answer important questions put to him about CIA mind control operations and related projects. He revealed that the CIA had indeed funded a series of such operations.

The revelations from the sub-hearing opened up many areas for subsequent investigation by investigative journalists and provided absolute proof that such work had been consciously carried out under the authority of successive administrations.

Senator Richard Schweiker asked Gottlieb about a notorious secret project known as RHIC (Radio Hypnotic Intercerebral Control) whereby people would have a miniature receiver implanted in them. Gottlieb answered that the technique did not exist. He continued, however. 'I am trying to be responsive to the terms that you used. As I remember it, there was a current interest, running interest, all the time in what effects people standing in a field of radio waves have, and it could easily have been that, somewhere in the many projects, someone was trying to see if you could hypnotise someone easier if he was standing in a radio beam. That could seem like a reasonable piece of research to do.' When Senator Schweiker added that he had heard testimony that radar (i.e. microwaves) had been used in animals to wipe out memory, Gottlieb responded. 'I can believe that, Senator.'[5]

The main advocate of these programmes was Edward Hunter, a CIA contract employee operating undercover as a journalist. He later became a prominent member of the right-wing John Birch Society.[6] The programmes in question were code named MKULTRA, MKSEARCH, MKACTION, MKNAOMI, ARTICHOKE and BLUEBIRD, which involved people being used as human guinea pigs in mind experiments. As a result of this increasing range of programmes, many subjects had lost their sanity and at least two people died. A letter from the CIA to the author states:

'The files of this agency do contain evidence that research sponsored by the CIA and involving human testing was conducted prior to 1963 in the field of behavioural control, using techniques involving hypnosis and drugs – primarily LSD – under Project MKULTRA and some related projects. The designator MKDELTA referred to a special procedure governing the use of MKULTRA materials abroad.'[7]

MKULTRA was not limited to the use of drugs alone. Sensory deprivation, religious cults, microwaves, psychological conditioning, psychosurgery, brain implants and several other areas of research were also gathered under the MKULTRA cover. In total it consisted of 149 sub-projects plus another 33 additional closely related sub-projects, all funded through the black budget.

Under the provisions of the Freedom of Information Act, 215,000 pages of records released by the CIA are merely records of the financial aspects of these programmes. They contain glimpses of evidence for the period when the CIA conducted its work through the Office of Security in 1953, and later through the Technical Services Staff (TSS) up to 1962. Several records are available from 1962 onwards when mind control research was transferred to the Office of Research and Development (ORD). However, from the 1950s to 1962 most of the original records, documents and research papers were deliberately destroyed.

Although in Senate Committee hearings during the 1970s some of the CIA's clandestine activities surfaced, a great deal more remained hidden in the military intelligence archives. Other Department of Defense departments were involved, as well as several private scientific institutions and laboratories working for the DoD and the CIA in the United States and especially in Europe.

One of the staunch theorists and believers in the use of hypnosis during warfare, George Eastbrook, secretly hypnotised two of his friends when trying to prove his point, whilst impressing guests at a party. He led the victims to believe the British Prime Minister had just arrived and the two spent over an hour conversing with their imaginary VIP guest. As the late Miles Copeland, a former CIA officer of some rank, said to a reporter. 'The congressional sub-committee which went into this sort of thing got only the barest glimpse.'[8]

The Mind Controllers

Footnotes

1. Vannevar Bush's memorandum to James Conant, Bush-Conant files, Office of Scientific Research and Development, S-1, Record Group 227, National Archives.

2. Leslie R. Groves, 'Now It Can Be Told' (New York, Harper and Row, 1962), pp 359-66.

3. The aide-memoir of Quebec agreement between Roosevelt and Churchill is in the Foreign Relations of the United States; The Conference at Quebec, 1944 (Washington DC: GPO), pp492-93.

4. Harry S. Truman, 'Memoirs' by H. S. Truman, Vol. 1, 1945: Year of Decisions (New York, Signet 1965), pp 20-21.

5. Human Drug Testing by CIA, p 202. Joint Hearing, Before the Select Committee on Health and Scientific Research of the Committee on Human Resources, US Senate. 95th Congress, 1st Session, 3 August 1977.

6. Edward Hunter is a veteran of the China theatre, which later produced personalities such as Richard Helms, Fred Crisman, Paul Halliwell and Mitch Werbell. Hunter coined the term 'brain washing'. See Miami News, 24 September 1950.

7. CIA letter to author, dated 19 October, 1990.

8. Robert Eringer, 'Secret Agent Man', Rolling Stone 1985.

Chapter Two

Unethical Experimentation

On 15 January 1994 under an order from President Bill Clinton, an Interagency Group on Human Radiation Experiments was created. John Deutch, Director of the Central Intelligence Agency at the time was a panel member of this group, which was set up with the aim of directing government agencies to look into unethical experiments conducted during the Cold War. John Deutch was also a panel member of the Advisory Committee on Human Radiation Experiments. Presenting the final report of their findings in October 1995, Chair Ruth R. Faden thanked Clinton, 'for his courage and leadership in appointing the Advisory Committee.'[1]

On 4 January 1994 James Woosley, then the Director of Central Intelligence, issued an Agency-wide order to search for 'possible CIA involvement in testing for the effects of radiation.' Following the Executive Order of 17 January 1994, the CIA established an in-house Human Radiation Experiments Steering Group to conduct a search. It was composed of representatives from all the CIA directorates, the DCI's office and from offices dealing with Congressional, legal, public, and historical issues. Woosley commissioned David Gries,[2] then director of the CIA's Center for the Study of Intelligence (CSI), to oversee the search.[3]

In the course of their quest, the CIA discovered documents that clearly suggested the Agency's involvement in human radiation testing. Despite this evidence, and despite the CIA's long history of involvement in unethical human experiments over several decades, they claimed that these records did not concretely prove the CIA's involvement. Through a carefully worded and classified memorandum, of 21 January 1994, David Gries focused the search on the question of whether the CIA had, 'deliberately subjected human beings to ionised radiation, whether in tests to determine the effects of radiation on human beings or in efforts to discover operational uses for radioactive substances or their emissions.' By narrowing the scope of the search, Gries enabled the Agency to circumvent its involvement with private contractors and laboratories which had been commissioned to conduct such research for them – damage limitation for any future implications and law suits that might follow.[4]

Guided by the narrow focus of Gries' memorandum, the CIA did not search specifically for information on a 1949 experiment known as Green Run. Nor did they seek out information on other intentional releases of radiation. Foreign intelligence information and reports that may have influenced other agencies to conduct experiments were duly passed over.

Subsequently, on 13 April 1994, the CIA issued a statement to the Advisory Committee that, following an electronic review of approximately 34 million documents, a manual review of 480,300 pages, and nearly 50 interviews,[5] 'no documents were found to date to suggest that CIA conducted experiments or operations using ionised radiation on human subjects.'[6]

The CIA also claimed that if such experiments were conducted, they were carried out by CIA contractors, with the CIA having no interest in them. Significantly, the statement also contained a CIA admission that, according to its records of the MKULTRA programme, it might have conducted such experiments.

The MKULTRA programme was a group of projects 'concerned with research and development of chemical, biological, and *radiological* materials capable of employment in clandestine operations to control human behavior.'[7] (emphasis added) One of the CIA's documents clearly states that, 'additional avenues to control the human behavior' were to include, '*radiation*, electro-shock, various fields of psychology, sociology, and anthropology, graphology, harassment substances, and paramilitary devices and material.'[8]

It is therefore clear from this evidence that the CIA was far from innocent regarding human radiation experiments. With input from numerous independent sources and researchers, as well as victims, the staff of the Advisory Committee made thirty requests for information and records in pursuit of potential leads to the CIA.

Documents from MKULTRA and several other projects clearly make references to the use of radiation as part of their research efforts. Additionally, at least one CIA officer attended the Department of Defense meetings in the early 1950s at which human radiation experiments were discussed in conjunction with atomic bomb tests.

The CIA's human behaviour control programme was chiefly motivated by perceived Soviet, Chinese, and North Korean use of mind control techniques. The CIA originated its first programme in 1950 under the name of BLUEBIRD, which in 1951, after Canada and Britain had been included, was changed to ARTICHOKE.

MKULTRA officially began in April 1953 as a clandestine funding mechanism for wide ranging research into human behaviour. Technically, it was closed in 1964, but some of its programmes remained active under project MKSEARCH well into the 1970s. MKULTRA was run by the Technical Services Staff (TSS), which is also known as Technical Services Division (TSD). The main purpose of these programmes was their potential use in espionage and covert operations.

In 1973, tipped off about forthcoming investigations, Richard Helms, then Director of Central Intelligence, ordered the destruction of any MKULTRA records. In 1976, in testimony to the Church Committee, Helms confessed that 'there had been relationships with outsiders in Government agencies and other organisations,' and that 'these would be sensitive in this kind of thing; but since the program was over and finished and done with, we thought we would just get rid of the files as well, so that anybody who assisted us in the past would not be subject to follow-up questions, embarrassment, if you will.'

The Church Committee did find some records during its investigation in 1976. However, it noted that the practice of MKULTRA at the time was, 'to maintain no records of the planning and approval of test programs.'[9]

It must be stressed that the focal point of MKULTRA was the use of humans as unwitting subjects. The CIA sponsored numerous experiments of this kind. An internal CIA investigation followed the death of Dr Frank Olson in 1953, after he had been given LSD.[10] Despite warning of the dangers of such experimentation the CIA persisted in this practice for at least another ten years.

Regardless of another report, by the CIA's Inspector General in 1963, recommending the termination of testing on unwitting subjects, Deputy Director for Plans, Richard Helms continued to advocate covert testing on the ground that, 'positive operational capability to use drugs is diminished owing to lack of realistic testing we are less capable of staying up with the Soviet advances in this field.'[11] On the subject of moral issues in connection with covert human experiments, Helms commented, 'we have no answer to the moral issue.'[12]

In response to a request filed by John Marks in 1977, under the Freedom of Information Act (FOIA), the CIA discovered additional MKULTRA records in financial files held by the Office of Technical Services. These had not been indexed under the name MKULTRA. The documents became the subject of hearings by Senator Edward Kennedy in 1977.

In 1963 a CIA Inspector General's investigation report on MKULTRA had stated that the programme was, 'concerned with research and development of chemical, biological, and radiological materials capable of employment in clandestine operations to control human behaviour', and that 'radiation' was one of the additional 'avenues to control the human behavior.'[13] The CIA was unable to provide any logical or convincing explanation for this to the Advisory Committee on Human Radiation Experiments.

The Committee members found a number of CIA documents on the 140 MKULTRA sub-projects with references to radiation. In sub-project 35, for example, the CIA secretly provided $375,000 for a new wing at Georgetown University Hospital in the 1950s, to be used in chemical and biological programmes. Dr Charles F. Geschickter, a Georgetown doctor, provided cover for the CIA's work, and with that money he funded the radioisotope lab and equipment.[14]

In sub-project 86, Dr Wallace Chan received CIA funds for research on polygraph machines and other means of establishing the veracity of agents. In an undated Memorandum for the Record, Chan proposed, 'artificial means of establishing positive identification' (known as covert marking) involving ionising radiation: namely, radioisotopes, with predetermined half lives, selectively implanted and/or injected; and radiologically opaque foreign bodies selectively implanted and/or injected into predetermined sites in the human body.'[15]

Backed by funds from the CIA, Dr James Hamilton, a CIA consultant under MKULTRA sub-project 140 (which later became MKSEARCH sub-project 3) was to set up and operate a so-called 'sleeper laboratory'. Instead, Hamilton used the funds to set up a lab in the Vacaville California Prison Medical Facility where he conducted tests on prisoners. In a letter from Hamilton to the Geschickter Foundation, dated 30 March 1965, outlining the funded work, Hamilton stated: 'we are now conducting a new series of experiments on 100 prisoner-subjects, in which radioactive iodine uptake of the thyroid and T-4 uptake of red cells, and several other measures which we have developed, are being related to previously studied variables.'[16] Today

Hamilton claims to have no recollection of ever having done any experiments on the prisoners.[17]

BLUEBIRD-ARTICHOKE documents make several references to ionising radiation. One CIA History Staff Memo describes an undated outline of ARTICHOKE research that lists, 'radiation' among many 'other fields' that 'have been explored', in addition to chemicals, hypnosis, and psychiatry. Another card file from the ARTICHOKE records on 'Radiant Energy' discusses the possibility of a 'sleep ray', stating that: 'it is possible that some newer field of radiant energy, some atomic particles, could be aimed at sleep centers in the brain, or at brain centers that inhibit the waking state. Sudden sleeping might be produced in this way, with an unwitting subject if the apparatus were worked from another room.'[18]

However, this proposal was rejected by Dr Webb Haymaker, an expert from the Armed Forces Institute of Pathology, on the grounds that, 'he doubted that any such approach, as by ultrasonic or other radiant energy, would ever be possible.'[19]

Another ARTICHOKE card file on 'Tracer Techniques', stated that Massachusetts General Hospital had developed a technique, 'for the tracing of radioactive material throughout the human body and particularly the brain.' It went on to say, 'Along these lines, several of our most important consultants have constantly urged exploration of the tracer techniques as a method of advancing ARTICHOKE studies.'[20]

MKULTRA sub-projects 17 and 46 involved the use of radio-isotope tracers on laboratory animals to study the effects of LSD. It is unclear whether similar radioactive tracers were used on humans in the course of the CIA's experiments with LSD, despite the knowledge that the CIA did use LSD on humans with one fatal casualty.

Available evidence shows that it was not only the CIA that was involved in clandestine human experimentation. From 1950 until the 1970s, the CIA collaborated closely with the US Army whilst conducting LSD and other chemical tests on humans.[21]

The majority of tests carried out on humans by the Army were conducted at Fort Detrick and the Edgewood Arsenal Research Laboratories (EARL), both in Maryland. The Army's key contractor for this research was Dr Albert Kligman, from the University of Pennsylvania. Some of Kligman's research for EARL, including the use of radioisotopic material, was conducted on inmates from Holmesburg Prison in Pennsylvania.[22]

In the mid-1960s, Dr Kligman founded the Ivy Research Laboratories (IRL). They became the conduit for EARL to perform experiments which they themselves could not conduct. EARL's records on human experimentation raised some serious ethical questions. They show that in 1971 the CIA provided EARL with $37,000 to test a classified glycolate compound, known only as EA3167. A potentially incapacitating psycho-chemical agent, EA3167 was tested on human subjects, including prisoners from Holmesburg Prison. One of the main objectives of the CIA in these tests was to synthesise radio-labelled EA3167.

In January 1975, a memo from the CIA Office of Inspector General shows that EA3167 was used on 20 human subjects, and that follow-up observations and examinations were conducted. Based on this document, the testing protocol was 'analogous' to that used by Ivy Research Laboratories.[23]

The CIA terminated its contract with EARL in 1973.[24]

During the course of the Department of Energy's recent investigations, CIA officials categorically denied that EARL's contract with the CIA ever used human subjects. In support of its claim, the CIA referred to its internal investigation in 1977 when Senator Kennedy's Hearings were convened.[25]

Records also show that the Department of Defense (DoD) was extensively involved in planning and conducting human radiation experiments in the context of their nuclear weapons programmes. DoD conducted most of this work in the late 1940s and early 1950s through DoD's Research and Development Board, which included several panels and committees.

For example, the Committee on Medical Sciences helped to formulate the policy that eventually led Secretary of Defense, Wilson, to issue a memorandum implementing the Nuremberg Code in 1953. The Code provided sufficient medical and ethical guidelines to safeguard the interests of volunteers in human experiments. However, for several decades afterwards, almost every US Government department and agency that was involved in human experiments ignored it.

Based on the DoD and National Archives records, the CIA was represented in at least eight meetings of the Committee on Medical Sciences.[26].

In 1952, Dr Clark Yeager, Chief of the Medical Division of the CIA's Office of Scientific Intelligence, attended a meeting during which the ethical issues pertinent to the use of humans in radiation experiments were discussed. He was later to act as one of the main advisors to the ARTICHOKE programme on foreign brainwashing research.

From the records it is clear that the CIA carried out research on radiological warfare (RW), and collected intelligence on Soviet attempts at RW. What is also clear is the collaboration between the CIA and the DoD, and their attempt to develop high-altitude balloons as a weapon that would disperse radiation over the Soviet Union in the mid-1950s. Yet, as early as 1953, the CIA concluded that the Soviet Union was not likely to develop radiological weapons.

In the early 1950s, the CIA proposed to the DoD and the Atomic Energy Commission (AEC) that a small scale radiological weapon be developed for use in unconventional warfare by guerrilla groups.[27] The CIA chaired the Joint Atomic Energy Intelligence Committee – the principal body responsible for monitoring the Soviet nuclear weapons programmes.

The Lawrence Livermore Laboratory (LLL), at the Department of Energy, has an extensive history relating to human experimentation,. Their collaboration with Britain's Atomic Energy Research Establishment and Harwell Laboratory expanded from 1972 until 1990.[28]

Based on a 1965 Memorandum of Understanding between the CIA and LLL (available to the public) it is clear that the LLL conducted experiments on behalf of the CIA, as a result of their association with the AEC and DoE.

In response to the Advisory Committee, the CIA denied finding any evidence, after the search of their classified files, that LLL did any human experiments on their behalf. Nonetheless, information available strongly suggests otherwise. Several individuals who were actively involved in human radiation experiments for DoD and AEC may also have performed work for the CIA.

Harold Hodge from the University of Rochester received funding from the CIA for LSD research.[29] Hodge also directed the Manhattan Project work at Rochester on the toxicology of uranium.[30] In another case, a CIA summary document to the Advisory Committee states that Dr Robley Evans: 'enjoyed a long history as a TSS/TSD consultant on radiation safety, radiation detection, and the use of trace radioactivity.'[31] Evans was also a professor at MIT, directly involved in human radiation experiments for the Atomic Energy Commission, DoD, and other agencies.

At a meeting in March 1995, three witnesses testified to members of the Advisory Committee that they had, indeed, been the subjects of the CIA's human radiation experiments under MKULTRA. Though the witnesses were unable to provide any documentation in support of their claims, they provided names of well-known individuals involved in the MKULTRA programme.

The Mind Controllers

As almost all of the operational records and documents of MKULTRA had been destroyed in 1973, the CIA was able to ignore the Advisory Committee's direct request for a further search of their records – rejecting the witnesses' claims as unsubstantiated, and denying any involvement in human radiation tests. Furthermore, the CIA is not prepared to facilitate the identification or the retrieval of non-government records that may be associated with government activity in human radiation experiments.

In conclusion it can be seen that, based on abundant documentary evidence and witnesses, the Agency has managed to cover-up yet another scandal in the breaching of its code of conduct.

Footnotes:

1. Letter of October 1995, to the Members of the Human Radiation Interagency Working Group from Ruth R. Faden, Chair of the Advisory Committee on Human Experiments.

2. David Gries is a veteran both of operations and analysis, and a proponent of reform in the Agency. He has written several articles in the CIA's in-house publication 'Studies in Intelligence'. See, for example, 'New Links Between Intelligence and Policy', in vol. 34, no. 2, Summer 1990, and 'Intelligence in the 1990s', vol. 35, no. 1, Spring 1991.

3. After David Gries' retirement in June 1994, John Pereira became the acting director of CSI, until Brian Lattel in September 1994 was appointed as the new director.

4. US departments continue a similar trend today. In response to a recent FOIA request for information on contracts for development of non-lethal weapons granted by the Department of Energy (DoE) to the University of California (UCLA), DoE advised me that such records are exempt from release on the grounds that they do not constitute agency (DoE) records – even though the contract has been granted by the DoE to UCLA. Application of the FOIA regulations in this area remains unclear and controversial. In a similar case where documents were originated by a

contractor for the US Army, the US Courts ruled for their release on the grounds that these were records created for a department, hence they constitute agency, not Army, records. I have appealed against the DoE decision.

5. The CIA provided the Committee with a list of 22 people who were interviewed. The Agency withheld the identities of the remaining individuals from the investigating Committee.

6. 'The Central Intelligence Agency's Search for Records on Human Radiation Testing', 13 April 1994.

7. Ibid.

8. 'CIA Inspector General Report of Inspection of MKULTRA', 14 August 1963.

9. Senate Select Committee to Study Government Operations with Respect to Intelligence Activities, 'Final Report', Book 1 – Foreign and Military Intelligence, 94th Congress, 2nd Session, 26 April 1976, Special Report No. 94-755 (Better known as the Church Committee Report). Also see Book 1, p. 406.

10. For several decades the CIA withheld from his family details of the death of Dr Frank Olson, who died after being given LSD. After several legal actions, the CIA resolved the matter in an out-of-court settlement, while denying any liability. The CIA settled in the same manner with several victims of Dr Cameron's 'Psychic Drive' experiments, of MKULTRA sub-project 68.

11. Ibid. Also see Church Committee Report, Book 1, p. 402.

12. Op. cit. 9.

13. 'Report of the Inspection of MKULTRA/TSD', 26 July 1963.

14. The Geschickter Fund for Medical Research served as the principal cut-out source for the CIA's secret funding of numerous MKULTRA projects.

Additionally, CIA tried to enlist the Atomic Energy Commission to co-fund the project by appealing to its interest in Geschickter's radiation research.

15. Wallace L. Chan, MD, 'Memorandum for the Record: Establishing and substantiating the 'bona fides' of agent and/or staff personnel through techniques and methods other than

interrogation', undated.

16. James A. Hamilton, MD, to Geschickter Fund for Medical Research, 30 March 1965 ('This is a request for a grant....').

17. Telephone conversation with the author, October 1996.

18. Advisory Committee on Human radiation Experiment [ACHRE], CIA record number CIA-071095-A.

19. Dr James H. Huddleson to Chief, Technical Branch, Office of Security, 'Conference with Dr Webb Haymaker', 4 November 1953.

20. Op. cit. 17.

21. Church Committee Report, Book 1, p. 395, states that one of the three principal functions of the Special Operations Division (SOD) of the US Army Biological Center at Fort Detrick was to conduct 'biological research for the CIA'. In early 1952, SOD agreed 'to assist CIA in developing, testing, and maintaining biological agents delivery systems. By this agreement, CIA acquired the knowledge, skill, and facilities of the Army to develop biological weapons suited for the CIA's use' – Church Committee Report, Book 1, p. 389. Many of the early CIA LSD tests were conducted at Fort Detrick.

In the late 1960s, much of work of MKSEARCH, at TSD (Technical Services Division) was transferred back to Fort Detrick. Dr Christopher Green, and Major Edward Dames played significant roles in the CIA's biological and chemical warfare development.

22. The 'Philadelphia Inquirer', 18 September 1977, cites a 1963 local news article describing an Army experiment at Holmesburg 'in which prisoners were to have limited areas of their skin exposed to small amounts of radioactive isotopes.'

23. Memorandum for Deputy Director for Science and Technology, 'OFTEN/CHICKWIT Revisited', 19 October 1978.

24. Scott Breckinridge, Memo to Inspector General, 'RD Research and Development for Intelligence Applications of Drugs', attachment on 'Influencing Human Behavior', pp. 2-3, 31 January 1975.

25. Op. cit. 7, and 'Memorandum for the Record: Trip Report/Edgewood Arsenal', 12 February 1975.

26. Names of the CIA representatives were listed on the roster of the transcripts of the first, third, fourth, fifth, tenth, thirteenth, fourteenth, and seventeenth meetings of the Committee on Medical Sciences.

27. CIA History Staff Memo, 1994, pp. 10-12.

28. 'In Vivo Calibration Studies Using Humans Administered Niobium-92, Barium-133, Palladium-103, Chromium-51, and Strontium-85. Human Radiation Experiments Associated with the US Department of Energy and Its Predecessors', US DoE, Assistant Secretary for Environment, Safety and Health, July 1995, p. 90.

29. John Marks, 'The Search for the Manchurian Candidate', Times Books, New York, 1979, p.118. 'Hodge's group found a way to put a radioactive marker into LSD.'

30. See J. Newell Stannard, 'Radioactivity and Health: A History', DoE Office of Scientific and Technical Information, 1988.

31. ACHRE's CIA-080994-A record, 'CIA Interview Notes of Persons Contacted Regarding Human Radiation Experiments', 1994. Although the CIA had formerly disclosed to the Committee information concerning Robley Evans, Brian Latell, Director CIA Center for Study of Intelligence, on 4 August 1995, sent a letter to Advisory Committee Chair, Dr Ruth Faden, stating that 'as a matter of policy, the Central Intelligence Agency can neither confirm nor deny the existence of contractual relations with either [Dr Robley D. Evans, or Dr Harold C. Hodge].'

The Mind Controllers

Chapter Three

The LSD Trials

It is not only the CIA that has been involved in mind control experiments. This chapter examines hallucinogenic-type drug experiments conducted by various elements of the US Army Intelligence community in conjunction with sections of the US Army Chemical Corps. Most of the related records have been destroyed. What follows is based upon the records salvaged from these programmes.

From the available records in the Intelligence Center at Fort Holabird, Maryland, and the Chemical Warfare Laboratories we know that a joint co-ordinated psychochemical drug project started in November 1957. The ground work for this joint project was supposedly conducted in the latter part of 1957 and early 1958. Discussion took place between officers of the Intelligence Board at Fort Holabird and the Medical Research Laboratories at Edgewood Arsenal in May 1958. Following a meeting on 3 June 1958, the President of the Intelligence Board sent an informal plan to the Medical Research Directorate of the Chemical Warfare Laboratories.[1]

The plan was entitled 'Material Testing Program EA 1279' and involved the use of LSD. It discussed the 'method of approach to prospective volunteers' who were to be selected from official personnel, based on their records that included security clearance information. It called upon a proper code of conduct for volunteers, requiring them to sign a security statement. The volunteers were to be examined physically and mentally prior to any testing.

The test programme on the first group of volunteers arriving at the Army Chemical Center (ACC) Edgewood, involved a specific emphasis on 'Unwitting test reaction'. A three day stay was required for the test to be carried out on the first group. After physical examination, those who were physically unfit were excused.

On the evening of the first day at ACC, the group met socially. Having studied their file, a trained interrogator was introduced to the volunteer. The purpose of the evening for the volunteers was to socialise. In reality the scene was set for each interrogator to try and elicit additional information from the volunteer under his control – simulating a diplomatic cocktail party where an attempt would be made to obtain classified information from unwitting subjects.

All drinks served to volunteers contained LSD. The interrogators then tried to extract extra-classified information about the volunteer's special duties at their place of service. Where and when necessary, the interrogators, without the knowledge of their subject, administered additional doses of LSD.

Facilities were provided for private meetings and interviews between each pair. Interviews held in the evening were to be compared with interviews held the following day, when the individual would no longer be under the influence of the drug. The volunteers were unaware of the 'interview' process. However, on the second day they were informed about the previous evening's events.

Experiments were conducted on further groups of volunteers at Edgewood to evaluate their ability to lie whilst under the influence of LSD. There were also 'Memory Impairment Tests', to assess the effects LSD had on the memory of the individuals; 'Specialized Motor Reaction Memory Testing', to evaluate the impairment of simple motor reactions after taking LSD; and 'Effect of Environment and Physical Condition Testing', evaluating the effect of LSD on those subjected to various environments and physical conditions, including total isolation and hostile interrogation situations. A further test 'Influence of Material Under Artificially Created Stress Situations', determined the ability of the subject to withhold information under unusual stress and the influence of LSD.

There is no evidence that these tests were approved at any level above the President of the Intelligence Board or Director of the Medical Research Laboratories at Edgewood. The only document available to the office of the Inspector General and the Auditor General, US Department of the Army, shows that the proposed plan was sent from the Intelligence Center to the Commanding General at Edgewood.

It was signed by the Adjutant General for the Center Commander, indicating that the Intelligence Center Commander may have approved the programme from the Intelligence Corps side.[2] However, the former Commander of the Intelligence Center, Richard S. Prather, in his testimony of 29 October 1979, admitted that he knew nothing about the plan, and it is possible that the letters were signed on his behalf. He further stated that although the Intelligence Board was located within his command, they usually reported directly to the Office of the Assistant Chief of Staff for Intelligence, (ACSI) Department of the Army, regarding subjects dealing with operational matters.[3]

The Intelligence Board Project Officer, William J. Jacobsen, supported Richard Prather's testimony. He added that it was his understanding that, at the time, no definite decision could have been made at Holabird to participate in these tests without the approval of ASCI.[4] Jacobsen's statement on this matter was not confirmed by former ASCI staff. Furthermore, no evidence was found showing that the Medical Research Laboratories obtained approval through the Chemical Corps, nor had the Surgeon General's Office checked or reviewed the plan. They had clearly overstepped the legal line.

The surviving records show that the experiments were conducted in two phases: the first series of tests from August to November 1958,[5] and the second from September 1959 to May 1960. Although there are no records of the exact number of volunteers used, from the travel orders and testimony, it would appear that 30 to 35 volunteers were involved. There are no records to indicate the number of times LSD was administered to each volunteer.

Importantly, none of the volunteers gave their 'informed consent' prior to receiving LSD. Furthermore, there was a deliberate attempt to deny the volunteers any information that would have permitted them to evaluate the dangers involved. The responsibility for this deliberate failure lies with the Intelligence Board, as the initiator, and the Medical Research Laboratories, as medical investigators. It was only after surreptitious administration of LSD that the volunteers were informed and briefed about the rest of the project.

These tests were conducted a few years after Dr Frank Olsen's death, the probable cause of which was the administration of LSD in his drink in November 1953. Dr Olsen had worked quite closely with the Army's Chemical Corps' Special Operation Division (SOD) at Fort Detrick. Records show that the US Army soon put lessons learnt from Olsen's death behind them and carried out tests as before.

According to the testimony of Charles L. Shirley Jr., one of the volunteers, made on 5 August 1975, the belief amongst most of the volunteers was that if they declined to participate in the tests it would have put them in immediate disfavour with their superiors.

After the first phase of Intelligence Corps experiments in November 1958, a letter from the Chief of Clinical Division at Edgewood to Commanding General Army Intelligence Center stated that all the initial work on the first phase was completed with rewarding results.

He further recommended that 'actual application of the material [LSD] be utilised in real situations on an experimental basis, if possible.'[6] It is hard to believe such a recommendation on a dangerous drug, with unpredictable results, being made after tests on only 35 volunteers.

On 21 January 1959 the US Army Intelligence Center gave the go-ahead to Edgewood: 'This headquarters has forwarded your letter to the Assistant Chief of Staff for Intelligence (ACSI), Department of the Army, concurring in your recommendation that that actual application of the material be utilised in real situations on an experimental basis.'[7] From the records available, a field test plan was prepared with Medical Research Laboratories' representatives and an Intelligence Board officer to aid interrogation.

Early in March 1959 the Director of Medical Research at Edgewood informed his superior, Commander of Chemical Warfare Labs, that the plan would be submitted to him shortly by the Intelligence Center.[8] The plan called for use of LSD on foreign nationals overseas. The Surgeon General's Office was the avenue chosen to rapidly implement the plan.[9]

On 9 April 1959, representatives from the Chemical Warfare Laboratory and the Intelligence Center briefed the Chief at Research and Development, Office of the Surgeon General on 'Material Testing Program, EA 1279', proposing field experimentation. He had shown reservations about approving the plan, but later informally notified Edgewood that the Surgeon General would reconsider if it was presented through the Assistant Chief of Staff for Intelligence (ACSI). The Intelligence Center sent the plan to the ACSI to be co-ordinated with the Surgeon General, and the latter 'concurred in the finding of the Chemical Corps and offered no medical objections to the field experimental plan.'[10] The Office of the ACSI ordered the Commander, US Army Intelligence Center (USAINTC) to prepare a detailed staff study about the test on overseas nationals and a report for ACSI. On October 15 1959, USAINTC sent the requested study to ACSI.[11]

On 8 August 1960, the 'Office of Assistant Chief of Staff Intelligence Liaison Team' was sent to Europe to brief the European intelligence community on the joint Intelligence Corps/Chemical Warfare Laboratories project for testing LSD and acquaint the G-2 US Army Europe (USAREUR) with the plan. The team consisted of three members: the action officer from the Office of the Assistant Chief of Staff for Intelligence of the Department of the Army (OACSI); the Project Officer from the US Army Intelligence Board at Fort Holabird (USAINTB); and another Project Officer from the US Chemical Research and Development Laboratories (USACRDL) at Edgewood.

It was left to the intelligence community in Europe to devise the details of the plan and provide the subjects for the proposed 'Field Test'. They were to be non-volunteer, foreign nationals. The Department of the Army was to be responsible for implementation under the watchful eyes of the Special Purpose Team (SPT).[12] Surviving records suggest that on 25 November 1960 the Deputy, ACSI and the G-2 USAREUR, informally agreed to the working relationship.[13]

On 7 December 1960, the USAINTC Project Officer, in the presence of representatives of the Chief Chemical Officer DA, and the Surgeon General's Office, briefed the ACSI.[14] His report shows that ACSI agreed to the plan because it would enhance conventional interrogation methods. Although little concern was voiced, the question of co-ordinating with other agencies such as the CIA and FBI was raised.

The final decision was to postpone such co-ordination until the European field tests had been assessed. Of ACSI the report records, 'His concern was that if this project is going to be worth anything it [LSD] should be used on higher types of non-US subjects and, as he put it – staffers.

This could be accomplished if the CIA was brought in.' ACSI also added that 'maybe the FBI should be informed and possibly join us to further develop the experimentation.'[15]

There is absolutely no evidence that this plan was approved by the Chief of Staff of the Army or any other officers higher than ACSI. Furthermore, there is no evidence that it was co-ordinated with the FBI, CIA or any other non-US Army department. In January 1961 the Chemical Corps sent an officer to become a member of the Special Purpose Team, joining the USAINTB project officer.[16] The new member, supposedly provided by the Surgeon General's Office, was a medical officer from Fort Totten, New York. (There is no documentary evidence of this assignment by the Surgeon General.)

On 28 April 1961 the Department of the Army EA 1279 (LSD) Special Purpose Team (SPT) departed for a 90 day field experimentation programme to Europe, 'Operation THIRD CHANCE'. The team consisted of an Army medical officer, a Chemical Corps EA 1279 project officer and the US Army Intelligence Center project officer representing OACSI. The objectives were: 'to confirm or refute laboratory findings (1958-60) in an effort to ascertain whether or not the EA 1279 technique could be employed as an aid to interrogation and whether or not the technique does enhance the exploitability of actual subjects of intelligence interest.'[17]

The sponsoring intelligence units had already nominated the subjects. They all came from a critical category and were considered 'unresolvable' through conventional interrogation or investigation techniques.

The subjects were brought, individually, to a prearranged operational site on the pretext that they were to undergo a physical examination by the SPT doctor. After being introduced to the members of the SPT socially, the subjects were surreptitiously administered LSD in drinks. Once the LSD had taken effect the group moved on to an interrogation room. The medical officer and psychologist were present throughout the interrogation in an advisory capacity.[18]

There were 11 experiments involving 10 individuals, all but one of whom were foreign nationals, Army intelligence sources or agents. The exception was a US soldier who was involved in the theft of classified documents. None of the subjects had volunteered, although one had agreed to take a 'truth serum' test.

The Special Project Team returned to the US in late July 1961. They concluded that there was an urgent need for advanced and unconventional techniques to improve the field capability of intelligence units where intensive special interrogations were required, and that LSD had a promising future in this area. Among their other recommendations were: 'A comprehensive field testing programme to be established in conjunction with appropriate associated US intelligence and security agencies for the scientific derivation of empirical data upon which to standardise the EA 1279 technique; and that future field experimentation utilise real subjects of actual cases for both research purposes and operational advantage.'[19]

There is no evidence that any part of THIRD CHANCE was presented to, or approved by, the Army Chief of Staff or the Secretary of the Army. From the evidence it is clear that from start to finish the project violated Department of Defense and Department of Army policies, as well as specific procedures set for chemical or medical research. Furthermore, the SPT used non-volunteers of foreign nationality in all but one case. Additionally, the use of the US soldier was operational rather than experimental. Finally, the flagrant disregard for Department of the Army policies and directives was the responsibility of the Assistant Chief of Staff, Intelligence, the Office of the Surgeon General and the Chief Chemical Officer.

After the return of the Special Project Team from Europe in December 1961, a decision was made by ACSI to explore the possibility of similar experiments in the US Army Pacific (USARPAC).[20] On 27 February 1962, the Intelligence Corps project officer briefed the

Assistant Chief of Staff, G-2, USARPAC about the LSD programme at his headquarters in Hawaii. 'The primary purpose of the field testing programme will be experimental research under actual operating conditions, verification of previous laboratory and field test findings regarding [LSD] technique and development of further data regarding operational employment of the material. Any operational gains accruing to individual cases selected for experimentation will be considered a collateral advantage.'[21]

The initial tests began on 20 April 1962. The programme was code named Operation DERBY HAT, and ACSI requested the Chief Chemical Officer to provide an officer as a member of the SPT for this phase.[22] The Chemical Corps assigned the same officer who had participated in Operation THIRD CHANCE.[23]

For reasons that are unclear, Operation DERBY HAT was aborted before LSD could be administered to any of the eight subjects chosen for it – seven foreign nationals and one US soldier. In a briefing on 10 April 1963, the Deputy of ACSI, DA ordered that no further field testing with EA 1279 be conducted. The reasons given were the lack of data, the inconclusive nature of the tests, and the legal, political and moral problems inherent in the use of EA 1279(LSD).[24]

In conclusion, over the course of two years, the Intelligence Corps used 30 to 35 humans in their LSD tests. The first experiments, surreptitiously administering LSD at a simulated social reception, were in direct violation of published Department of Defense and Department of Army policies. No records are available for the majority of the volunteers nor for the tests themselves. Records were deliberately destroyed to protect the identity of the participants in these operations. The use of LSD was stopped as of 10 April 1963 in the US Department of the Army. However, these operations opened new avenues for other US agencies – including allies of the US government – to continue research using LSD on unwitting human subjects.

The Mind Controllers

Footnotes

1. US Army Chemical Warfare Laboratories (ACC), MD. Letter to Commanding General, US Army Intelligence Center, Fort Holabird, MD. Subject: Proposed Plan for Field Experimentation with EA 1279, dated 19 March 1959.

2. US Army Intelligence Center, Fort Hollabird, letter to Commanding General, US Army Chemical Center, Edgewood, MD. Subject: Material Testing Programme EA 1279, dated 28 April 1958.

3. Disposition Form by a Medical Research Laboratory staff member. Subject: Comments on 'K' Material Testing Programme Proposed from USAINTC, dated 27 March 1958.

4. Testimony of Lt. Col. (Retd.) William J. Jacobsen, 29 August 1975.

5. US Army Intelligence Board, letter to Chief Medical Research Directorate, Chemical Warfare Laboratories. Subject: Transmittal of Planned Worksheet, dated 3 June 1958.

6. Medical Research Laboratories, letter to Commanding General, US Army Intelligence Center. Subject: Material Testing Programme EA 1279, dated 14 January 1959.

7. US Army Intelligence Center, Letter to Commanding General, US Army Chemical Research and Development Command, Edgewood. Subject: Material Testing Programme EA 1279, dated 21 January 1959.

8. Disposition Form from Director of Medical Research to Commander, US Army Chemical Warfare Laboratories. Subject: CIC Test Plan, dated 6 March 1959.

9. USAINTC Letter to ACSI, DA. Subject: Staff Study: Material Testing Programme EA 1279, dated 15 October 1959. (Includes a reference to ACSI-SC letter, 27 July 1959, requesting study.)

10. Ibid.

11. Ibid.

12. Report of trip of OACSI Liaison Group re Material Testing

Programme EA 1279, dated 26 August 1960.

13. US Army Chemical Corps Research and Development Command, letter to Commander, US Army Chemical R and D Laboratories. Subject: Material Testing Programme EA 1279, dated 25 January 1961. Enclosure 2, Material Testing Programme EA 1279. Phase 1, Background and Summary to date. Undated.

14. Ibid. – enclosure 4. Fact sheet by OACSI/ODSMCI Security Division. Subject: Material Testing Programme EA 1279, dated 9 December 1960.

15. Ibid.

16. Ibid. without enclosure.

17. Project Officer Report to ACSI. Subject: Report of Trip and Activities of the Department of the Army EA 1279 Special Purpose Team re: Operation 'THIRD CHANCE', dated 6 September 1961.

18. Ibid.

19. Reference to letter, ACSI-SC. Subject: Material Testing Programme EA 1279, dated 29 December 1961.

20. Memorandum for Record. Subject: Policy and Operational Factors involved in the conduct of Field Experimentation of EA 1279, dated 1 March 1962.

21. ACSI letter to Chief Chemical Officer. Subject: Material Testing Programme EA 1279, dated 28 March 1962.

22. US Army Chemical Corps Research and Development Command Letter. Subject: Material Testing Programme EA 1279, dated 6 April 1962.

23. ACSI letter to USAINTC. Subject: Material Testing Programme EA 1279, dated 9 April 1962, with attached Memorandum for Record.

24. ACSI, DA, Memorandum for Record. Subject: Material Testing Programme EA 1279, dated 12 August 1963.

The Mind Controllers

Chapter Four

The Buchenwald Touch

In mid-November 1993, following six years of research, 42 year old Eileen Welsome produced a series of articles examining the lives and deaths of five people – a railroad porter, a house painter, a carpenter, a politician and a homemaker – who had been used as human guinea pigs by the US Department of Energy. Appearing in the Albuquerque Tribune, a newspaper in sparsely populated New Mexico with a 35,000 circulation, the articles sparked interest among major national newspapers.

On 7 December 1993, Secretary of Energy Hazel O'Leary ordered her department to open classified files covering projects that had involved the use of human beings as guinea pigs since the war. She was unaware of the enormity of the programme and the legacy of despair it had left behind. She ordered 32 million secret documents to be reviewed for release to the public and pledged to compensate the victims. She thought she was alluding to approximately 800 people, mostly mentally retarded or terminally ill. Her department received 10,000 calls in the first week.

'As you may know, the Department [of Energy] is committed to making as much radiation research information as possible available to the public. To this end, a major project has been initiated, Department wide, to identify relevant documents.' So wrote Dennis B. Diggins, Chief of Freedom of Information and Privacy Acts Branch (DoE) to me, enclosing an index listing the programmes and projects involving human testing. The index itself runs to 150 pages. The DoE conducted studies dating back to 1942, concerning the effect of plutonium on children as well as adults. Talbot, Newton and Warner wrote their findings in a report after injecting two healthy men with plutonium;

Toohey, Cacic, Oldham and Larsen used intravenous injection of plutonium to study the concentration of plutonium in the hair;[1] after administering plutonium to their victims, Moss and Gauter tried to study the 'additional short-term plutonium urinary excretion.'[2] Others exposed their victims directly to plutonium;[3] and still other scientists, after intoxicating their victims with radioactive material, conducted autopsies to study the plutonium concentration in the tissue.[4] All these tests had the support and funding of the DoE.

In some instances their victims were chosen from hospital patients. Between 1953 and 1957 William Sweet and his associates at Massachusetts General Hospital in Boston, injected at least 11 terminally ill cancer patients with uranium-235. According to the Albuquerque Tribune, at least six of the patients were not about to die and had been diagnosed wrongly. Furthermore, two were suffering from conditions disrupting the metabolic pathways that the investigators were examining.

Albert Stevens, a house painter from Healsburg, California, was believed to be suffering from terminal stomach cancer. On 14 May 1945, he was injected with what was described later as 'many times the so-called lethal textbook dose' of plutonium. On May 18 a biopsy showed that he suffered from an ulcer and not cancer. In July 1947, Elmer Allen, an African-American railroad porter was believed to be suffering from bone cancer. According to records, he was perhaps the last victim to be injected with plutonium.

A report dated 29 April 1946, describes how the Navy injected two hospital patients with a radioactive substance to determine a technique for measuring the rate at which human blood and organs would rid themselves of radioactive material. Over a period of weeks in 1945, blood, faeces and urine samples indicated the speed of discharge. By placing a Geiger counter in the vicinity of the liver, gall bladder, thyroid and brain, the researchers tried to discover a crude estimate of how much of the chemical had lodged in these places.

In another series of experiments during the 1940s, pregnant women were given cocktails of radioactive material in order to study their effects on the foetus. The Department of Health conducted tests that involved feeding more than 800 pregnant women a 'cocktail' laced with radioactive iron isotope in order to chart how it is absorbed in the body. The tests were conducted at Vanderbilt University's free pre-natal clinic in Nashville, funded partly by the Tennessee Department of Health.

In March 1951 a report in the American Journal of Obstetrics and Gynaecology details the iron absorption in pregnant women – but fails to mention monitoring the long-term effects of radiation on pregnant women or their children. Vanderbilt officials conceded that they do not know if the women were told of the possible effects of radiation or even if they knew they were being given radioactive pills. All the records were destroyed in 1970. (A follow-up study published in 1969 in the American Journal of Epidemiology concluded that three children born to women who took the pills during these tests almost certainly died.)

Dr Joseph G. Hamilton, a neurologist at the University of California Hospital in San Francisco, and his colleague Dr Robert S. Stone, continuously encouraged the Atomic Energy Authority (the DoE's predecessor) to use radioactive material on humans. In April 1946 Hamilton injected plutonium into a boy with terminal bone cancer and, despite the Army's advice in December to immediately stop this work, sent the Army a secret report on radiological warfare. In it he described how radioactive material could be used as a weapon of destruction, either on targeted individuals or communities as a whole: 'The inhalation of 10 millicuries of the unseparated fission product mixture is estimated to be a minimum lethal dose for the average adult human. It is presumed that lethal injury will arise in the main through pulmonary damage rather than bone marrow destruction. The oral ingestion of at least 100 millicuries of such a mixture would be required to produce lethal injury.'[5] To eliminate an entire community Hamilton suggested: 'One of the principal strategic uses of fission products will probably be against the civilian population of large cities. It can be well imagined the degree of consternation, as well as fear and apprehension, that such an agent would produce upon a large urban population.'[6]

Hamilton made a number of proposals for the elimination of large populations, among them 'fission product aerosols to subject urban populations to fission production poisoning by inhalation.'[7] In 1949, the Army conducted the first of six tests of radiological munitions at Dugway Proving Grounds in Utah, as part of the 'pilot experiments on a fairly large scale' of Hamilton's aerosol idea. (Hamilton chaired the panel of experts who advised the Army on the tests.)

In 1950 he wrote to the Atomic Energy Commission about the possibility of finding healthy human volunteers to inhale near-lethal doses of radioactive aerosols, admitting that his experiments have 'a little of the Buchenwald touch.' He considered the 'contamination of a very small reservoir by a large amount of [radio]active material', but concluded that 'the effectiveness of such a procedure would not warrant the use of the large amount of material required.'[8] He suggested that such programmes should be carried out by the Chemical Warfare Service with the collaboration of other interested branches of the Army and Navy.

In 1964, despite Hamilton and Stone's 'Mengelism', Dr Stone was awarded the AEC's citation for 'inspired effective and pioneering leadership.' (Hamilton died in 1957 of a rare form of leukaemia, almost certainly caused by exposure to radiation, at the age of 49.) The DoE involved other Department of Defense compo-

nents in its research, and shared its findings with the
Department of the Army, Navy, Air Force, and even
NASA and the Veterans Administration. Each of these
departments had, and still have, keen military interest
in what they term Radiological Warfare (RW).[9]

An Atomic Energy Commission document discovered by Sandra Marlow, lists more than 100 sites in the
Bay state, including the Massachusetts Institute of
Technology (MIT), Harvard University, Waltham's
Fernald State School and several Boston hospitals,
where human tests were conducted. Tests on the children in Fernald School in Waltham MA are particularly
alarming. In 1947, 17 retarded teenagers at the school
were given radioactive contaminated meals in order to
trace the amount of radioactive iron absorbed in the
body. Between 1954 and 1956 scientists affiliated with
MIT Radioactive Centre fed radio-tagged milk to 32
mentally retarded children at the school. (Team leader
Robert Harris believed that such experiments would
best succeed if the subjects were in a confined location and under medical supervision.)

Austin LaRocque and Charles Dyer, both former
students at the Fernald State School, told a panel
headed by Senator Edward M. Kennedy and
Representative Edward Merkey that at that time they
could not read or write and the researchers failed to
obtain the full consent of them or their guardians.

From December 1962 to April 1963 Harvard
researchers, sponsored by the US Public Health
Service, fed radioactive iodide to 760 mentally retarded children at the Wrentham State School – some were
as young as one year old. (It is unclear how much
radioactive substance was given to them or whether
any of their parents or guardians were informed.) The
tests were carried out in order to determine the 'mini-
mal effective doses' required to suppress thyroid. Such
tests had only one purpose: they would aid in the
development of counter-measures against fall-out from
a nuclear bomb explosion.

The Mind Controllers

At times, entire communities were the unwitting subjects of the experiments. In response to my request concerning these US programmes, projects and tests using humans to turn radioactive fallout into a weapon, the DoE's Albuquerque Field Operation Office informed me that, 'Los Alamos conducted the RaLa [Radioactive Lanthanum] open-air experiments from 1944 through 1961. The purpose of the programme was to test weapon designs using conventional high explosives.'

Often referred to as hydrodynamics tests or simply hydrotests, the RaLa experiments were critical to designing and developing nuclear weapons.'[10] By the end of 1946, 71 RaLa experiments had been conducted in Bayo Canyon. In 1950 the Air Force Cambridge Laboratory, using a B-17 bomber, conducted four atmospheric tracking tests of radioactive emissions in New Mexico. Sensors were used to measure the concentration of radioactive material in the clouds as well as the radiological activity in the atmosphere. Communities living in the area were not informed of the tests. According to the DoE's document, it would have taken at least two weeks before the radioactivity would have died down in the atmosphere. Many records pertaining to this particular programme, including those generated by other Department of Defense channels as part of its co-operation with DoE, remain classified.

In another series of experiments, civilians as well as military personnel were exposed to body radiation tests. Between 1963 and 1976 Carl Heller, from the University of Oregon and Pacific Northwest Foundation, exposed the testicles of 67 prisoners at Oregon State Prison to ionising radiation. Similar experiments were conducted by C. Alvin Paulsen (Heller's protégé) of the University of Washington, on the testicles of 64 inmates at Washington State Prison between 1963 and 1970 in order to test the effects of radiation on fertility.

According to documents, the US government carried out radiation experiments in at last 33 veterans' hospitals during the Cold War. Ironically, according to the Department of Veterans Affairs, 'the purpose of the experiments was to determine the effects of radiation on military [personnel] and to aid in diagnoses and treatment of some patients.' The VA eventually acknowledged in December 1993 that military patients in at last 14 facilities were victims of these experiments.

Reynolds Electrical and Engineering, a long time contractor to the Department of Energy, was ordered to provide their records for review and declassification. After denying any knowledge about 'any human experimentation at the NTS [Nevada Test Site]' with the exception of 'instances in which the US Environmental Protection Agency (EPA) would spray their field in Area 15 with tritium', the General Manager, D.L. Fraser, finally conceded in his letter of 7 December 1993 to Bruce Church, Assistant Manager for Environment, Safety, Security and Health of the Nevada Operations Office of the DoE, that: 'In the area of human experimentation, several types of studies were found which merit discussion.'[11]

Fraser attached several categories of records to his letter. Attachment 2 included documents on plutonium and uranium studies, funded by the DoE with no direct participation by the Nevada Test Site. Attachment 3 included study reports on samples of fallout from 4500 feet east of the detonations of the Small Boy Event (nuclear test), funded by the DoE and conducted by the University of Chicago and the Argone Cancer Research Hospital.[12]

Attachment 4 was of particular interest, relating to Special Military Projects. As Fraser put it: 'These were psychological studies which occurred at the Nevada Test Site.' One report was labelled, 'Relation between Information Gain and Attitude Change': a study of participants in Exercise Desert Rock V (A-bomb program) by Berton Wingrad, March 1954. Studies were conducted on several occasions on military participants who apparently volunteered to view a detonation at certain distances from ground zero. In one occasion during the Upshot-Knothole series of nuclear tests in 1953, the military subjects were told to stand only 2000 yards from ground zero. In another experiment during 'Operation Blumbbob' (a mispelling of Plumb-bob) in 1957, five subjects were stationed directly below the point of detonation of the high altitude John Event (nuclear test).

Oscar Rosen of Salem, commander of the National Association of Atomic Veterans, estimates that 450,000 to 500,000 military personnel were exposed to radiation during nuclear tests. In addition, hundreds of thousands of civilians were within 50 miles of nuclear tests held in Nevada, or intentional radiation releases at Hanford Reservation in Washington and Idaho National Engineering Laboratory.

Another two interesting snippets were included in attachment 7. The first was a memorandum by Dr Charles L. Dunham, dated 13 May 1966, entitled 'Use of Human Volunteers in Biomedical Research'; the second was a letter from Lloyd Bruton to the AEC, dated 26 March 1953, in which he offers himself to be used as a 'human guinea pig'. Attachment 8 also revealed the Stanford Research Institute's involvement in human testing under the title 'Fallout and Radiological Countermeasures'.

Contrary to the impression created by the DoE, these tests were not just carried out in the 1940s and 50s. As late as 1973, Federal scientists exposed prisoners in Oregon and Washington State to increased doses of radiation in order to determine the risks faced by a high-radiation environment. Argus Makhijiani of the Institute for Energy and Environmental Research in Takoma Park, Maryland, suggests that: 'There is plenty of evidence that some of these tests were designed to give the US an offensive radiological capability.'

Revelations continue to emerge, through declassified documents, relating to the US Government's use
of human guinea pigs in radiation experiments. They
provide a gut-wrenching illustration of how the government can turn on its own population; sinking to a form
of barbarity whilst disguising it through the secrecy
intrinsic in the national state of security.

A White House task force is now investigating but
despite Secretary O'Leary's pledge to compensate the
victims, a ruling from the Supreme Court stated that
even when someone's constitutional rights are violated by the Federal agencies, these agencies cannot be
liable for providing any compensation. 'If we are to
recognise a direct action for damages against Federal
agencies, we would be creating a potentially enormous
financial burden for the federal government', Justice
Clarence Thomas wrote for the court.

Whether Britain and other countries played a role
in testing is unclear. '[The US] Department of Energy's
focus on these studies is overly restrictive, if they are
trying to obtain a full picture', says Daniel Burnstein,
president of the Centre for Atomic Radiation Studies.[13]
It is known that the DoE made several shipments of
isotopes to other countries for research, although it is
not clear for what they were used. AEC documents
show isotopes were sent to Argentina, Australia,
Belgium, Brazil, Canada, Chile, Columbia, Cuba,
Denmark, Egypt, Finland, Mexico, the Netherlands,
New Zealand, Norway, Pakistan, Peru, Spain,
Switzerland, Sweden, Turkey, South Africa, the UK and
Uruguay. In response to my inquiry, the British Atomic
Weapons Establishment denied that Britain had any
participation in radiation tests using humans.[14]

However, the Albuquerque Operations Office of the
DoE has provided evidence to the contrary. In their
released index of 'Human Studies Project Team
Reports', they list 'United Kingdom Atomic Energy
Authority Research Group Report: Studies of the
Toxicology of Plutonium'.[15]

The Mind Controllers

Footnotes:

1. Toohey, Cacic, Oldham and Larsen, 'The Concentration of Plutonium in Hair Following Intravenous Injection'. Health Physics, vol. 40: pp. 881-886, 1981. DoE Albuquerque Field Office Record.

2. Moss and Gautter, 'Additional Short-term Plutonium Urinary Exertion Data from the 1945-47 Plutonium Injection Studies', in Proceedings of the Department of Energy Workshop on Radiobioassay and Internal Dosimetry, Albuquerque, New Mexico, 20-22 January 1986.

3. Voltz, Stebbings, Hempelman, Haxton and Tork, 'Studies on Persons Exposed to Plutonium'. International Atomic Energy Authority, SM-224508, 13-17 March 1978.

4. Fox, Tietjen, McInroy, 'Statistical Analysis of a Los Alamos Scientific Laboratory Study of Plutonium in US Autopsy', Health Physics, Vol. 39 pp. 877-892, 1980.

5. 'Radiological warfare(s)': From Joseph G. Hamilton MD to Colonel K.D. Nicholas, 31 December, 1946, p. 3.

6. Ibid. p. 4.

7. Ibid. p. 5.

8. Ibid. p. 5.

9. In their letter of 16 February 1994, the Office of the Command Judge Advocate, US Army, informed me that my request for further records on this subject (human radiation experiments) has been passed to a higher command.

10. Bayo Canyon The RaLa Programme - record released to author on 8 April 1994.

11. Record released to author by DoE, Washington, on 9 March 1994.

12. LeRoy, Rust and Hasterlik, 'The Consequences of Ingestion by Man of Real and Simulated Fallout'. Health Physics, Vol. 12, pp. 449-473.

13. 'Records hint at US role in worldwide radiation tests,' Nick Tate, Boston Herald, 24 January 1994.

14. Atomic Weapons Establishment, letter of 9 February 1994 to author. AEW further informed the author that 'We have consulted the Ministry of Defence who are the custodians of much of our early history, and they have confirmed this' – i.e. that no radiation tests involving humans were conducted.

15. It was initially held by the DoE Albuquerque Operation Office, New Mexico, and was made available on 2 March 1994.

The Mind Controllers

Chapter Five

Secret Partnership

The notorious Moscow trials of 1937 during Stalin's regime caused consternation in the West, notably the speed with which the defendants in the People's Court, like Cardinal Mindszently of Hungary, confessed to crimes against the State. A later CIA memo said: 'Characteristics and manner of the defendants, and formulation and delivery of the confessions, have been similar in a large number of cases as to suggest factitious origin.'[1]

The evident incongruities prompted the CIA's Office of Scientific Intelligence (OSI) in 1949 to undertake an 'analysis of foreign work in certain unconventional warfare techniques, including behavioural drugs, with an initial objective of developing a capability to resist or offset the effects of behavioural drugs.'

Preliminary phases included a review of drug-related work at institutions such as Mount Sinai Hospital, University of Illinois, University of Michigan, Detroit Psychopathic Clinic, Mayo Clinic, and National Institute of Health (NIH). There was also an extensive review of foreign literature, particularly from the Soviet Bloc. This programme became Project BLUEBIRD, with the objectives of:

'(a) discovering means of conditioning personnel to prevent unauthorised extraction of information from them by known means,

(b) investigating the possibility of obtaining control of an individual by application of special interrogation techniques,

(c) memory enhancement, and

(d) establishing defensive means for preventing hostile control of Agency personnel.'[2]

This evolved to become the blueprint and bible of other mind control programmes and psychological operations adopted in the West for decades afterwards. The Korean War – which started in June 1950, almost a year after the beginning of Project BLUEBIRD – was influential. The return of brainwashed POWs encouraged Western intelligence to delve even further into mind control techniques.

On 1 June 1951, in the course of a top secret meeting held in the Ritz Carlton Hotel in Montreal, Britain and Canada joined forces with the Central Intelligence Agency to: 'Research into the general phenomena indicated by such terms as – 'confessions', 'menticide', 'intervention in the individual mind', together with methods concerned in psychological coercion, change of opinions and attitudes, etcetera.'[3] The participants were senior figures in the military, intelligence and scientific communities including: Dr Haskins, Dr Donald Hebb (a Defense Research Board University Advisor in Canada), Dr Ormond Solandt (Chairman, Defense Research Board, Canada), Dr Dancy (MI6 - UK), Dr N.W.Morton (a staff member of Defense Research Board, Canada), Dr Tyhurst, Commander Williams, and Sir Henry Tizard (Chairman, Advisory Council on Scientific Policy and the Defence Research Policy Committee, Ministry of Defence - Britain).[4]

This was the beginning of close co-operation that lasted throughout the BLUEBIRD, ARTICHOKE and MKULTRA projects. The accidental survival of some records from these programmes, in particular MKULTRA, provides documentary evidence of the Canadian Government's involvement. However, information on Britain's participation remains sketchy due to continuous British Government secrecy.[5 & 6]

Minutes from the Ritz Carlton meeting include: 'At the opening of the discussion, there was an attempt to lay out some of the particular interests with which this group might concern itself in reference to the general problem described above [confessions, menticide, intervention in the individual mind – sic]. In this regard, the following points were noted:

'(i) That the concern with change of opinion was with reference to individuals primarily, and to groups only so far as the change of public opinion as a whole or propaganda might involve concepts and particular facts that led to increased phenomena of conversion of attitude.

'(ii) The means of methods; physical, neurophysical, psychological or other – that might be used to include change of opinion or conversion of attitude in the individual.'[7]

Within the space of three months after this top secret gathering, Bluebird was re-designated, as a 1975 CIA report records: 'in August 1951 Project BLUEBIRD was renamed Project ARTICHOKE, [and] in 1952 was transferred from OSI to the predecessor organisation of the Office of Security. OSI did retain a responsibility for evaluation of foreign intelligence aspects of the matter and in 1953 made a proposal that experiments be made in testing LSD with Agency volunteers.'

'Meanwhile, the emphasis given ARTICHOKE in the predecessor organisation to the Office of Security became that of use of material such as sodium pentothel in connection with interrogation techniques and with polygraph.'[8]

In an attempt to conduct 'Experimental Studies of Attitude Changes in Individuals', 'Sir Henry Tizard, Dr Ormond Solandt and the CIA granted contract X-38 to Dr Donald O. Hebb from the McGill University in September 1951.'[9] The project focused on the use of sensory deprivation (SD) and isolation for the eliciting of information in the course of deep interrogation. Hebb believed that sensory deprivation would induce dramatic changes in behaviour and attitude. The first 'subjects used were student groups and each was paid $20 per day (24 hours) for as along as (they) could continue with the experiment.'[10]

The experimental conditions for volunteer students in comparison to other 'victims' of SD were markedly different. Volunteers were provided with an air-conditioned room, comfortable bed and good food during the period of the experiments, as well as a panic button to use whenever they decided to terminate the experiment. They wore translucent goggles, forcing them to see blurred light: 'The subject was not to talk except when asking to hear the recorded propaganda or when doing minor tests given to him by the experimenter. In other words the subject was in perpetual isolation.'[11]

Volunteers were apparently not subjected to any propaganda that would adversely influence their political or religious beliefs: '(This) was thought unwise, and for the protection of the individual (the) only propaganda material used (concerned) such relatively innocuous topics as ghosts, poltergeist, extrasensory perception and the Lamarkian theory of evolution.'[12] Despite these concessions, several of the volunteers began to have unusual visual and auditory hallucinations. Many found themselves unable to distinguish between waking and sleeping stages.

The work of Dr Macworth of the Applied Psychology Unit of the Medical Research Council at Cambridge, England was considered. He had produced data on the effects of monotony and boredom on individuals during periods of isolation.

The existence of other similar programmes, and a high level of co-operation between the three countries was confirmed by Dr Solandt. Canadians making such a contribution may have helped them to obtain information from the US and the UK.[13]

Solandt said in a letter: 'Hebb's research to date has given some indication that significant changes in attitude can be brought about by use of propaganda under condition of isolation. In addition, [Hebb] has shown that there is a significant decrease in intellectual efficiency under such conditions, and marked increase in susceptibility to hallucination.'[14]

When the information concerning the SD tests were leaked and published in the Montreal Star, the Gazette, and the Toronto Star in 1954, Dr Solandt tried his best to conceal the facts: 'When earlier this month it became evident that some information on this project was in the hands of the press, it was decided that while it would be injudicious to reveal the original purpose of the project, it would be equally unwise to refuse to give any information at all. A compromise was therefore arranged whereby the project was described, but entirely from the point of view of possible implications for civilian or military operational situations in which a display had to be watched, a moving vehicle controlled etc.'[15]

Due to Donald Hebb's contribution to mind control programmes, the CIA funded Ewen Cameron's Psychic Drive Project through MKULTRA sub-project 68.

At the time Hebb was the head of McGill's Psychology Department, and a close friend and colleague of Cameron. The 'Psychic Drive' programme left behind a legacy of despair for participants, and years later numerous victims sued both the Canadian Government and the CIA.

Dr John C. Lilly, another psychologist, studied sensory deprivation in 1956 by immersing volunteers in a tank of lukewarm water. The subjects had to wear a particular type of facemask enabling them to see only blurred light. Under total silence, and lack of any stimulation, the subjects suffered mental disturbances. The maximum time a volunteer could tolerate these conditions was only three hours. The volunteers reported feelings of unreality and a tremendous loss of identification. They did not know where they were, who they were, or what was happening to them. Due to this enormous mental pressure most of them abandoned the experiment.[16]

Experiments in SD soon proliferated. Donald Hebb was granted further contracts by the US Air Force.[17] Biderman and Zimmer (1961) conducted extensive research on interrogation techniques using SD, also funded by the USAF.[18]

The Mind Controllers

Vernon, another researcher on this subject, admitted in the acknowledgement to his book 'Inside the Black Room': 'The entire project was made possible by a generous grant-in-aid of research given by the Office of Surgeon General of the US Army, and by National Science Foundation.' Unashamedly, he went on to add: 'While our goal is pure knowledge for its own sake, we have no objection to someone's use of that knowledge.'[19]

The official paperwork shows there were three aspects to further SD research. Firstly, the requirement for more experimental studies to research the basic effects of SD and sleep deprivation. Secondly, the use of these techniques in interrogation. Thirdly, their utilisation in special warfare techniques by specialised troops.

It was the accumulation of that knowledge, by the military, which led to the modern Psychological Operations (psy-ops). It subsequently enabled the British government, on 9 August 1971, to unleash one of its largest deep interrogation experiments. Though plausibly denied by the Government at the time as a political exercise against terrorism, the experiments used torture and sensory deprivation on Irish internees. Some were made to stand with hoods over their heads while electronically generated noise was played through speakers or headphones. They were naked, half-starved and abused.

Lord Parker admitted that the SD methods used on the Irish internees were 'techniques developed since the War to deal with a number of situations involving internal security. Some or all have played an important part in counter-insurgency operations in Palestine, Malaya, Kenya and Cyprus and more recently in the British Cameroon (1960-61), Brunei (1963), British Guyana (1964), Aden (1965-66), and Persian Gulf (1970-71).'[20]

The military use of Psy-ops was clearly gathering pace. NATO's first symposium on defence psychology was held in Paris in 1960, a couple of years after F.H. Larkin, from the Army Operation Research Establishment in Britain, travelled to Fort Bragg. There he addressed a conference on human factors in military affairs based on 'British Psychological Warfare Techniques in Malaya'.[21]

In 1963, the US Department of Defense held its first world-wide Psy-ops conference, outlining twenty-eight specific areas of expertise, with Britain as one of its main participants. The unprecedented operations in Northern Ireland, marked by repeated breaches of various articles of the Human Rights Convention, prompted Amnesty International, the Association of Legal Justice, the Committee on Administration of Justice (Northern Ireland), as well as the European Court of Human Rights to intervene – adding their voice and concern to the plight of the victims.[22] After undergoing horrendous experiments, a great number of internees suspected of terrorism were subsequently released without any charges.

Most of the original fourteen victims of the first phase were made to sign a paper that they had no complaints about their treatment during interrogation. Those who signed the paper implied they did so because they were frightened, or because they did not 'understand the contents'.[23] Several suffered from deep psychological scars for years afterwards, and some continue their suffering. Others died shortly after these experiments and a few attempted suicide during their captivity and interrogation.[24]

An Amnesty International report later stated: 'As a result of its investigation, the Commission concludes that the ill-treatment used in these cases clearly amounted to brutality, and (we) disagree with the Compton Committee (the official investigation) when they state: "Where we have concluded that physical ill treatment took place, we are not making a finding of brutality on the part of those who handled these complaints (paragraph 105)."

'The officials who gave evidence to the Compton Committee also said that one of the purposes of the hooding and continuous noise [white noise] was to increase the sense of isolation, so it is obvious that the methods used during interrogation in depth were therefore intended to affect the recipients psychologically.[25]

'In the opinion of the Commission, the interrogation in depth especially, but also the 'special exercises', constitute violation of Article 5 of the Universal Declaration of Human Rights and Article 3 of the European Convention for the protection of Human Rights and Fundamental Freedoms.'[26]

A memorandum submitted by Amnesty International to the Parker Committee on Interrogation Procedures, stated: 'It is because we regard the deliberate destruction of man's ability to control his own mind with revulsion that we reserve a special place in our catalogue of moral crimes for techniques of thought control and brainwashing. Any interrogation procedure which has the purpose or effect of causing a malfunction or breakdown of a man's mental processes constitutes as grave as assault on the inherent dignity of the human person as more traditional techniques of physical torture.'[27]

In 1970, at the World Conference on Religion and Peace, held in Kyoto, Japan – where representatives of all the world's religions were present – the following declaration was made: 'The torture and ill-treatment of prisoners which is carried out with the authority of some governments constitutes not only a crime against humanity, but also a crime against the moral law.'[28]

Britain was rapidly regarded as an expert in psychological operations, and has regularly been invited to give demonstrations and hold military seminars, notably at Fort Bragg, Carolina; Fort Huachuca, Arizona; and Bad Tolz, Germany. For a time they also instructed the PIDE (the Portuguese secret police).

However, to their embarrassment, it was discovered that since an Army coup they had been educating Latin American guerrillas in counter-insurgency and torture techniques. Communist members of the Portuguese Army were active in these groups.[29]

Britain holds its main psychological operation courses at Ashford in Kent, Catterick in Yorkshire, Bradbury Lines (The SAS camp in Hereford) and Old Sarum in Wiltshire, where psy-ops courses for RAF officers are held. About 16 men and women take part, typically consisting of Green Jackets, SAS, Royal Marines and Royal Artillery, together with staff from the Ministry of Defence (MOD) and the Foreign Office (FO).[30]

Sensory deprivation experiments were also carried out by what were known as Control Units in Wakefield and Wormwood Scrubs prisons. The British Home Office kept their very nature and existence secret. In August 1974, the Control Unit at Wakefield became the first to receive inmates. The concept was to break the will of troublesome prisoners using a modified version of SD.

The Sunday Times' Insight Team uncovered the existence of these units and their purpose in October 1974. As a result of adverse publicity and severe criticism, the UK Government was forced to disband them.

Done over a period of six months, the 'treatment' generally occurred in two phases. Sensory deprivation was the main focal point. Over the first 90 days a strict solitary confinement regime with almost no communication was applied. No conversation between the prisoner and guards was allowed, only gestures being permitted. If this appeared successful, the victim was allowed limited communication. If not, phase one would be repeated.

With the victims left psychologically scarred, and no positive results to show, Dr Pickering, ex-Director of Prison Medical Services, admitted in a BBC 'Man Alive' programme (20 May 1976) that, 'Control Units were a mistake.' It is ironic considering he was in charge when John Masterson, the first inmate, was subjected to this mental torture in 1974.

However, Roy Jenkins, Home Secretary at the time, supported these units and their operations. 'I am satisfied that the safeguards and procedures are such that the trained staff of Wakefield are able to maintain a careful and caring watch on the progress and condition of prisoners in the Control Unit.'[31]

A year later he remained adamant: 'I am satisfied that allegations, which have received considerable publicity, of sensory deprivation, cruelty and brutality in the unit, are completely unfounded and that the Governor and staff have conducted themselves in a commendably professional manner.'[32] The fate of the victims was ignored.

What had started in the Ritz Carlton Hotel in 1951, reached full fruition in 1971 with the Ulster guinea pigs. As Professor Robert Daly[33] stressed: 'The whole SD process in Northern Ireland was a package deal. Being awaken in the middle of the night, being beaten, confused as to your whereabouts, lied to and insulted, was all part of the 'unfreezing process' through which your psychological defences were broken down, and terror and humiliation were induced. Hence, the photographing in the nude, being forced to urinate while running, refusal to allow toilet visits, the sadism and abuse.

'Meanwhile the psychological functions of the body were being disturbed by the very low non-existent intake of calories, high temperature caused by sweating which could lead to dehydration, coupled with the cold at night, sleep deprivation and loss of sense of touch. The whole experience was a package. Whether you want to call it interrogation in depth or brain washing is academic. The aim of the treatment was to cause temporary psychosis, temporary insanity, which was a severe psychological injury liable to having lasting consequences'.[34]

As part of its mind control operation, Britain, like the CIA, used hallucinogenic drugs such as LSD on unwitting subjects. This included Irish internees interviewed by Amnesty International: 'Mr. Murphy alleges he was given tea and says that after drinking he saw images on the wall.'[35] 'Mr. Bradley alleges he suffered from hallucination after drinking a cup of tea.'[36]

To quote Garland E. Burrell Jr, Article 22 of the Universal Declaration of Human Rights guarantees 'the free development of personality.' But despite this and 'in spite of the various United Nations provisions concerning the personal integrity of individuals, no state is expressly precluded from altering the mental process of its nationals.'[37]

'The price of freedom is eternal vigilance,' said Albert Camus. Nowhere is this more clear than in the protection of our most precious human right, the freedom of the mind.[38]

Footnotes:

1. CIA memorandum 'An Analysis of Confession in Russian Trials', 1950. Also, see 'Are the Coniform Countries Using Hypnotic Techniques to Elicit Confessions in Public Trials' By; Irving L. Janis; US Air Force Project Rand Memorandum, 25 April 1971.

2. 'Behavior Drugs, and Testing', 5 February 1975, CIA Document.

3. Documents from the collection of the Manuscript Division, Library of Congress.

4. Tizard, Sir Henry Thomas, born 23 August 1885, GCB, AFC, FRS, LLD, Dsc, ScD, and holder of other titles (see Who is Who 1951, and Who is Who 1951-1960).

5. op. cit. 3.

6. In 1973 several key documents on the CIA's mind control programmes were destroyed on the order of Richard Helms, the CIA Director.

7. op. cit. 3.

8. op. cit. 2.

9. 'Confidential' letter, Dr Ormond Solandt, 3 August 1954.

10. ibid.

11. ibid.

12. ibid.

13. ibid., and Dr Solandt's conversation with author.

14. Letter to 'The Minister', Ormond Solandt, 25 January 1954.

15. ibid.

16. John C. Lilly, 'Mental Effects of Reduction of Ordinary Levels of Physical Stimuli on Intact Healthy Persons', Psychological Research Report 5, 1966, pp. 1-9. Also, see, Bexton et al., 'The Effects of Decreased Variation in the Sensory Environment', Canadian Journal of Psychology, vol. 8, 1954, 99. 70-76.

17. National Defence Headquarters [Canada] letter to author, dated 18 April 1994. Also, see D.O. Hebb et al., 'The Effects of Isolation Upon Attitudes, Motivation and Thought'. 4th Symposium, Military Medicine I, Defence Research Board, Canada, Dec. 1952 (Secret), and D.O. Hebb and W. Heron, 'Effects of Radical Isolation Upon Intellectual Functions and The Manipulation of Attitude', 4th Symposium, Military Medicine I, Defence Research Board, Canada, December 1952 (Secret).

18. Biderman, Zimmer, 'The Manipulation of Human Behaviour', Wiley, New York, 1961.

19. J. Vernon, 'Inside the Black Room: Studies of Sensory Deprivation', Penguin 1966.

20. Parker Report, Cmnd. 4901 (HMSO), para. 10.

21. F.H. Lakin from Army Operational Research Establishment (AORE), Britain, described the British Psychological Warfare research in Malaya between 1952-55. He was in charge of a nine man research team responsible to AORE, and the Research Division of the Director General of the Information Services [then the Federation of Malaya]. For six months two men from the Operational Research Office of John Hopkins University, Maryland, worked closely with his team, plus an Australian

Army psychologist.

22. Also see: (1) 'Repression Trade – (UK) Limited', How the UK Makes Torture and Death its Business, by Amnesty International, British Section 1992; (2) 'Submission to the United Nations Committee Against Torture', for consideration during the Committee's scrutiny of UK Government's Report. Committee on the Administration of Justice (Affiliated of the International Federation of Human Rights), 13 November 1993; (3) 'A Submission to the United Nation's Human Rights Committee', Containing Comments on the Forth Periodic Report by the United Kingdom of Great Britain and Northern Ireland to the Human Rights Committee under Article 40 of the International Covenant on Civil and Political Rights, by committee on the Administration of Justice, June 1995.

23. Report Of An Enquiry Into Allegation of Ill-treatment in Northern Ireland, Amnesty International, p.26.

24. For a more detailed account of the fate of the internees see 'The Guinea pigs', John McGuffin.

25. op. cit. 23, p.36.

26. Ibid.

27. op. cit. 23, p. 38.

28. Findings of The World Conference on Religion and Peace, p. 31.

29. In answer to a Parliamentary Question, Archie Hamilton, the British Minister of State for Defence listed 100 countries to which UK provides military training of various types, including Portugal, and other countries with notorious track records in violation of Human Rights, e.g. China, Chile, Iraq, Uganda, South Korea, Egypt, Turkey. He fails to place Cambodia on the list – See John Pilger's 'Cambodia: Year Ten'.

30. 'Precis 6: Psyop unit – General', Training Report, Senior Officer's Psyop Course, Royal Air Force, Old Sarum, Salisbury, Wiltshire, UK, Feb. 14/18, 1972. A British document devoted to the organisation and equipment of psy-ops unit, both at head-quarters, and broken down into subsections: Consolidation Psy-ops; Counter-Insurgency uses and their use in peacetime, as

well as details of deployment of psyop units in UK. Also, 'Technical Report of the Senior Officers' Psyop Course Held at RAF Old Sarum, 14-18 Feb. 1972'. This course clarifies the parallel nature of British psy-ops with that of the US Army's. Among people that have addressed these courses are: Keith Belbin, of Coleman, Prentice and Valery [Advertising Agency] on recruitment. Peter Bartlett on target analysis with reference to the Chinese use in Hong Kong. R.M. Farr [a psychologist from British Psychological Society] on attitude change, and B.R. Johnston on information policy in low intensity operations, mainly in Northern Ireland.

31. House of Commons [British Parliament] 14 November 1974.

32. House of Commons, 24 October 1975.

33. Prof. Robert Daly, expert in sensory deprivation. A graduate from Dublin University, Rep. of Ireland. Instructor in psychiatry at the University of North Carolina. Later a lecturer at Edinburgh University before taking post at the University College, Cork, Rep. of Ireland.

34. Robert Daly; 'Psychiatric After-effects of Irish Prisoners Subjected to Ill-Treatment and Torture', New Scientist, 5 August 1976.

35. op. cit. 23, p.14.

36. op. cit. 23, p. 23.

37. Garland E. Burrell, Jr., 'Mental Privacy: An International Safeguard to Governmental Intrusion into the Mental Processes', 6 California Western International Law Journal.

38. Alan Scheflin, 'Freedom of the Mind As An International Human Rights Issue', Human Rights Law Journal, vol. 3, 1982.

Chapter Six

Human Trials in Britain

The Nuremberg trials revealed the extent of Nazi Germany's mind control experimentation on Jewish concentration camp prisoners as well as prisoners of war. As a result of the trials, 23 German doctors were convicted, and an injunction was brought to the effect that humans should never be used in such a fashion again.

As we have already seen, neither the behaviour of the accused at the Moscow show trials (at which they confessed to crimes they palpably had not committed), nor the accounts given by POWs from the Korean War, were regarded as a warning. On the contrary – such trials only served to attract the interest of the Western intelligence agencies, inspiring them to research and develop methods of controlling and altering the human mind.

In 1953, Dr Frank Olsen, a scientist working for the CIA, was found dead on the pavement outside a New York Hotel. The CIA quickly actioned a cover up of the circumstances surrounding his death; questions remained unanswered, and the whole case remained shrouded in mystery until 1975, when it was finally revealed that Olsen had been one of many people unwittingly given LSD. He had been part of the Agency's experiments with the drug and LSD had allegedly been a contributory factor in his suicide.

In an article in the Mail on Sunday in 1998, Kevin Dowling disclosed that this account was also a cover-up, the story allegedly designed to mask a murder.[1] Dr Eric Olsen, son of the victim, explained to me in a telephone conversation that he shared Dowling's view. In 1994, his father's body was exhumed, following a court order and a team headed by James Starrs, Professor of Law and Forensic Science at the National Law Center at George Washington University examined the corpse. The first autopsy, allegedly carried out by the CIA, claimed that the body had suffered cuts and abrasions caused by Olsen crashing through the windowpane of the hotel room from which he supposedly jumped. This second autopsy found no evidence of such cuts and abrasions, but did find a haematoma (or bruise), unrecorded at the first post-mortem examination, on the left-hand side of Olsen's skull, most probably caused by a heavy blow, probably a hammer, before the fall from the window.

Based on the available evidence, Professor Starrs therefore suggested that the most probable cause of Olsen's death was homicide and not suicide.[2] His report suggested that Frank Olsen was murdered because he was considered a security risk to the CIA's highly sensitive and top secret mind control programmes.

As a biochemist, Olsen had worked in the US Army's Special Operation Division at Fort Detrick, Maryland since 1943. During the Cold War era, like many of his colleagues, he provided his services to the CIA in their mind control programmes, under the direction of Dr Sidney 'The Gimp' Gottlieb.

The US Army's programmes on the use of LSD[3] and an array of other chemicals, and their effects on the human mind, encouraged the CIA to embark on the biggest series of programmes and projects in mind control.

As we have already seen, during this period, the CIA sought the assistance and co-operation of other Western countries. On 20 April 1950, the Director of the CIA, Roscoe Hillenkoetter gave the go-ahead to the CIA's Project BLUEBIRD. A year later, in April 1951, the CIA began liaison with the army, navy, and the air force to prevent duplication of their efforts.[4] Two months later, the Ritz Carlton Hotel meeting in Montreal, Canada, took place and the CIA invited Britain and Canada to join forces.

As already outlined, there were discussions about facilitating 'confessions','menticide' and psychological coercion.'[5] The participants at the Ritz meeting reveals a lot about the nature of the agenda; Hebb and Solandt were naturally present, but Commander Williams may have been the representative of the British Navy[6] and Drs. Haskins, Dancey, and Tyhurst were probably the representatives of the CIA.[7]

Although Frank Olsen did not attend, he was already playing a key role in the mind control programme. Officially, MKULTRA was established on 13 April 1953, at Richard Helms' suggestion, and with Allen Dulles' (DCI) approval as 'ultra sensitive work'.[8] However, the operational wing of MKULTRA, known as MKDELTA, had begun in 1952. Its mission was to find out how to use chemical and biological weapon ingredients to alter the human mind.

The CIA's Clandestine Services was in charge of MKDELTA, which often used non-Americans in its experiments abroad. In 1952, the CIA initiated yet another programme through the Special Operations Division (SOD) of the US Army's Biological Research Center at Fort Detrick, Maryland to produce biological weapons for the CIA's use. This was called Project MKNAOMI.[9] Through this, the SOD developed an array of deadly substances for the CIA.[10] It has been established that Frank Olsen worked on these projects, and that between May 1950 and August 1953, he visited Porton Down in England, and as well as centres in France, Germany, and Norway.[11]

Increasingly unhappy about the effects of some of these experiments on humans, Olsen began to show signs of distress. As acting chief of the Special Operations Division for some months during 1952-53, he had access to all information concerning the development of the arsenal of toxic substances in the CIA.[12] After a trip to Paris and Norway, Olsen told his boss, Lt. Colonel Ruwet, he was so unhappy that he would prefer to be discharged or fired rather than carrying on with his work. This led to a memo being issued within Fort Detrick initiating an investigation into a 'possible breach of security after a trip to Paris and Norway.'[13] It was decided that Olsen knew too much.

Unbeknown to Ruwet, Olsen had already expressed his anxiety and disillusionment to Dr William Sargant, a Harley Street psychiatrist, who had been appointed by the British Government to co-operate with the US agencies in their mind control programmes.[14] Whether Sargant reported this matter to the CIA is not clear but, on Tuesday 23 November 1953, Olsen told Ruwet that he was 'all mixed up'. Seriously worried about the danger he would talk, Ruwet decided Olsen needed 'psychiatric attention.'[15]

After an emergency meeting with Gottlieb and Robert Lashbrook, Gottlieb's deputy, it was decided to send their 'patient' to Dr Harold Abramson in New York, an allergy expert and immunologist who was not formally trained in psychiatry. He was chosen because of his top-secret clearance with the CIA. After a discussion, Olsen accepted this decision, and Ruwet left him with Lashbrook. By now Olsen was quite certain the CIA was 'out to get him'.[16]

On 28 November 1953, Olsen's body was discovered on the pavement outside the Startler Hotel, New York having apparently thrown himself out of the thirteenth floor window. Nine days earlier, it is known that Gottlieb had spiked his drink with LSD but whether this was actually a factor in his death is now highly debatable.

After Olsen's death, in collaboration with the CIA's findings, Abramson wrote 'Olsen was in a psychotic state with delusion of persecution.'[17] The CIA made sure Olsen's widow, Alice, received full pension, but in 1975, the Rockefeller Commission condemned the CIA's cover-up and granted Mrs Olsen an apology and $750,000.

Alice and her son Eric Olsen were invited to the White House, where President Ford officially apologised for the CIA's actions. Throughout these years, Ruwet kept close contact with Alice Olsen, and became a close family friend and confidant. Whether Ruwet's concern for Mrs Olsen was an act of remorse remains unknown. The CIA on Project ARTICHOKE has now released hundreds of records and some coincide with the period when Dr Olsen was making repeated trips into Europe. A memorandum of 12 February 1952, originally classified secret refers to a conversation between the writer of the memorandum and another person. The CIA deleted both names. The following paragraphs, though in garbled English, are rather interesting:

'3. [Deleted] followed the writer a long document which apparently was merely a proposal for extensive 'Artichoke' both here and abroad and involved the outlay of approximately [deleted]. This plan more or less provided for the establishment of a laboratory in the United States (somewhere locally) and a large working area overseas.

'4. [Deleted] proposal seemed to be along the following lines:

'– OSI would recruit or have already been promised medical men, and scientists, etc. who would be available for the application of the latest possible techniques of all types to overseas subjects.

'– These techniques would be trained and produced by various agencies in the United States as [deleted].

'– These men would be a sort of super-expert, combining psychiatry, psychology, and medical knowledge and would tackle the subjects in the field.

'– The subjects would be primarily individuals [deleted] or individuals whom the Agency wished to do away with. [Deleted] subjects that there were [deleted] or all types where plenty of subject material could be had.

'– The very latest 'ideas' would be used including electroshock, lysergic acid, drugs, electroencephalograph, hypnosis, etc., etc.

The Mind Controllers

'– The old 'Bluebird' idea of an interrogation team would, of course, be done away with since these experts could administer the drugs, carry on interrogation, and handle the whole work themselves, apparently on an individual basis.'[18]

How many victims of these CIA programmes were subjected to these 'techniques' remains unclear.

In June 1964, Sid Gottlieb renamed MKULTRA, MKSEARCH.[19] The programme's mission was now to deal with seven sub-projects, mostly concerning the development of chemical and biological substances that would disorient, discredit, injure and even kill targets.

Many unwitting subjects fell victim to these programmes. Using various National Institute of Mental Health hospitals and facilities, Dr Harris Isabel ran an Addiction Research Center in Lexington, Kentucky, using LSD and a host of unproven drugs. Particularly appaling was Dr Isabel's tendency to target black and gay inmates for experimentation.

Many other groups used unwitting subjects in extensive behavioural control tests, using various chemical substances; these included: a group headed by Dr Bob Hyde's in Boston Psychiatric Hospital, Carl Pfeiffer at the University of Illinois Medical School, Harold Abramson at Mt. Sinai Hospital and Columbia University in New York, Louis Joylon West at the University of Oklahoma, and not forgetting Harold Hodge and his group.[20]

Similar events were taking place in Britain at the time, although details are sketchy. There is a brief reference in Peter Wright's book 'Spycatcher'. He notes that 'the whole area of chemical research was an active field in the 1950s', and he refers to a joint MI5/MI6 'programme to investigate how far the hallucinatory drugs lysergic acid diethyalmine (LSD) could be used in interrogation, and extensive trials took place at Porton'.[21] (Porton Down is the site of Britain's biological and chemical weapons research centre.)

Wright gives no date for this, but from the context he appears to be referring to the 1950s – the period when Olsen was visiting Porton Down. In an article I wrote for Lobster 26 in December 1993, I revealed that Dr Graham Pearson, Director of the Chemical and Biological Defence Establishment (CBDE), had written to me admitting that between 1961 and 1972, 72 servicemen volunteers had taken part in LSD trials in the UK. I also drew attention to reports in the Sunday Telegraph which reported that 'dozens of servicemen say they were tricked into painful chemical experiments at the government's Porton Down test centre by being told they were helping with research into the common cold.'[22]

In 1966, two major scientists, Dolores McMahon, a Senior Scientific Officer and C. Gordon Smith, Director of Porton Down, used terminal leukaemia patients at St. Thomas' Hospital in London. Apparently with their consent, the patients were deliberately injected with the lethal Langut and Kyasanur Forest virus. They were told that it might counteract the high levels of white cells in their blood. Four patients died, and two developed encephalitis.

In 1968, Eric Hadden, then Director of Porton Down, admitted in a BBC interview that CS gas was tested on 'aged people, asthmatic people, young people.'[23] In his letter to me in October 1993, Dr Pearson stated that up to 200 human trials were taking place at that time. In the 1950s and 60s this number would undoubtedly have been far higher.

Survivors of some of these early tests are still alive. Lance Corporal Mick Roche, now in his mid-50s, was asked to inhale nerve gas through a face-mask. He now suffers from chest problems, hypertension and what his doctor describes as 'mysterious premature ageing'. He was one of a group of ten subjected to these tests.

Another man now aged 60, suffers from blindness and eye pain. In 1951 he took part in trials which exposed his eyes to nerve gas. A former aircraft fitter in the navy, he also suffers from shakes, and an uncontrollable muscle ailment similar to Parkinsons Disease. He was a teenager when he took part in the test, and he claims that he was never warned about possible long term effects.[24]

On 31 July 1995, I wrote to Dr G.D. Coley, Director of the CBDE, enclosing a 38 page list of chemical and biological warfare substances, and asking him to identify those substances which CBDE had conducted or were conducting any kind of research and development with. On 11 August 1995, Dr Coley responded somewhat reluctantly, nevertheless marking the relevant items on the list. He identified no less than 390 groups of substances, among them: amphibian toxin, anthrax, anti-human immunodeficiency virus, bacterial toxins, biological bombs, micro bomblets, botulinum toxin, radiological weapon cloud transport, cholera, gas gangrene, cobra toxin, Congo Crimean haemorrhagic fever, cytotoxin, defoliants, DNA virus, lassa fever, greenmonkey virus, methantrophic bacteria, monkey pox, neurotoxins, plague, poxvirus, rabies virus, resistant tickborne virus, riot control agents, smallpox virus, tetanus toxin, toxin weapons, tuberculosis, typhoid, yellow fever – and the list continues.

Among this colourful list of substances, there remains yet another category which are listed only by name and number, and about which nothing is known, such as: BPL, BHA, blue27/b bomb, freon pe65702a, JEDS, SAEB, tc-83, td-1 agent, nl-1 agent, and many more.

In another letter, dated 21 June 1995, in response to my inquiry concerning the use of chemical biological agents in populated areas, for example the London Underground,[25] Dr Coley wrote: 'As we stated in our letter of 31 May, studies after 1955 involved the use of non-pathogenic simulants. Your letter refers to trials in London Underground. Studies, which had no generic name, involving simulants were conducted in 1963-64.'

It still remains unclear which tests were conducted prior to 1955, and what kind of chemical or biological agents were used. However, Dr Coley in his letter of 31 May 1995, provides a taste of the trials which took place prior to 1955: 'Between 1948 and 1955 several trials involving the use of pathogens were conducted off the Scottish coast and in the Caribbean '[26]

The sad truth is that like the Americans, the British State pursued a policy of employing ill-informed and unsuspecting civilians, service personnel and foreigners as guinea pigs. What has been described above is surely just the tip of an iceberg.

Footnotes:

1. Kevin Dowling, 'The Olsen File: A Secret that could destroy the CIA', Mail On Sunday (Night and Day section) 23 August 1998, and several conversations with Mr. Dowling.

2. Telephone conversation with Dr Eric Olsen, 20 October 1998; plus exchanged E-mails. In his memoir, the former SAS member Peter Stiff discusses forms of assassination and describes 'an old trick popular with the various government security services throughout the world.' 'I would knock on his door. When he answered I would club him, sweep him bodily to the window, and throw him out of headfirst.' See Lobster 32 p. 11.

3. See Chapter 3.

4. Document released to author in 1991 by the CIA on the ongoing origins of the creation of ARTICHOKE, and its contents.

5. Document whose only identification mark is a stamp saying it came from the collection of the manuscript division, Library of Congress.

6. Possibly Eric Charles Williams, in 1951 Director of Operational Research at the Admiralty.

7. The only documented result of this meeting was the award of contract X-38 to Dr Donald O. Hebb, from McGill University to conduct research in sensory deprivation. On 25 January 1954 Ormond Solandt, Chairman of the Canadian Defence Research

The Mind Controllers

Board, apparently in response to some Canadian press attention, wrote to an unidentified 'Minister' in the Canadian Government explaining that the Defence Research Board had awarded Hebb the contract research at McGill University in September 1951, and that it had 'originated from discussion among Sir Henry Tizard, representatives of the US Central Intelligence Agency, Dr Hebb .and myself in June 1951.' Like the document cited in note 5, this document came from the Library of Congress and has no other identification marks. Solandt's comment that the meeting was with 'representatives of the US Central Intelligence Agency' suggests that the three unexplained doctors on the list were the 'representatives of the US Central Intelligence Agency.'

8. Memorandum from ADDP Helms to DCI Dulles, dated 3 April 1953, Tab A, pp. 1-2.

9. Summary Report on CIA Investigation of MKNAOMI, Report Book I, pp. 360-63. Also see Kennedy Subcommittee Hearings on Biological Testing Involving Human Subjects by DoD, 1977.

10. Francis Gary Powers, the U-2 pilot captured by Soviet Union, carried one such toxin concealed in a silver dollar, and did not use it.

11. Documents released to Olsen's son and stamps on his father's passport. Information from a phone call with son. A glimpse of what was going on in Norway, with US money, was given in 'US and Norway 'used insane for Nazi-style tests'. The Times 29 April 1998, which claimed 'the American authorities financed 4,000 experiments on humans from 1944 to 1994' in Norway.

12. John Marks, 'The Search for the Manchurian Candidate', (Allen lane, London, 1979), p.77.

13. See Dowling, note 1, confirmed by Olsen's son. It may not be a coincidence that Stanley Glickman, an American who was unwittingly dosed with LSD in Paris, had this done to him in 1952 – and probably by Gottlieb.

14. See Dowling, note 1 above, Sargant was the author of 'Battle for the Mind: the mechanics of indoctrination, brainwashing and thought control', (Heinemann and Pan, London, 1957 and 59).

15. Kennedy Subcommittee, see note 12.

16. Ibid.

17. Kennedy Subcommittee note 10, pp. 394-403.

18. In a document dated 3 November 1960, the CIA set out to achieve the following effects using hypnosis: induce deep trance in an unwitting subject; induce deep trance rapidly, i.e. within seconds; produce indefinitely durable amnesia concerning the trance; produce indefinitely durable control of future behaviour through post hypnotic suggestion, including behaviour in conflict with the subject's normal pattern.

19. Origins of MKSEARCH is described in CIA's document 449, dated 8 April 1964, and document S-1-4 untitled. Also see, document 450, dated 9 June 1964, wherein Richard Helms recommends that MKULTRA to be renamed as MKSEARCH, as a new charter for 'Sensitive Research Programs'.

20. Substantial volume of records were released to the author by the National Institute of Mental Health (NIMH) on the work of Isabel and many others, named in this article. Also see CIA document 24 July 1953, Memo; Liaison and Security Officer/TSS Subject No. 71; an account of the Chemical Division in NIMH94; CIA document 37, dated 14 July 1954, and several others released by the CIA. These were among 700 pages of documents I supplied this year to Del Walters of the American TV company ABC for a documentary on this subject. The programme was broadcast on 4 and 8 November 1998.

21. Spycatcher p. 160.

22. Three years later The Daily Telegraph reported on 1 February 1996 that LSD had been tested on British troops in the 1960s; Also see Sunday Telegraph 2 November 1997.

23. Information from an Observer Films programme proposal, 'In the National Interest', 4 January 1997. The company approached me for help with a documentary on LSD research in Britain. Their information was shared with me in return.

24. Ibid.

25. 'The Day Germ Warfare came to Tooting Broadway', The

The Mind Controllers

Independent, Tuesday 28 March 1995.

26. In his letter of 31 May 1995, Dr Coley stated that 'Trials involving the use of biological agents were chiefly carried out by the Microbiological Research Establishment and its predecessors. The MRE closed in 1979.' He added; 'Studies undertaken since 1955 involved the use of non-pathogenic simulants such as Bacillius globigii and Escherichia coli which were judged not to present a risk to health. The work was conducted in order to assess the potential hazards of BW attack and to evaluate detection systems.'

Chapter Seven

Victims of Dargle Cottage

Anthony and Doreen Verney had recently retired. After a lifetime of hard work, they had high hopes of living out their days in peace and tranquillity in a small cottage in Kent. However, it was not meant to be; their dream was soon shattered by a nightmare experience when they became unwitting 'guinea pigs' in a mysterious experiment.

My careful and thorough research has failed to unearth anything to question the honesty, integrity or even the patriotism of this elderly couple. The Verneys are but one of several examples I have encountered in my experience who have come forward despite having lost everything, including their health, and spoken up with bravery about their frightening ordeals.

As will be seen, cases like the Verneys' make it all too important to bring to justice those dark forces that operate with legislators' immunity. These cases also remind us of the urgent need for a Bill of Rights in the UK as well as freedom of access to information to a much greater degree than is possible at present. For, the leprosy of secrecy has long eroded democracy in Britain today.

The Verney's torture began in Autumn 1983, and the results of all attempts at redress on their parts can be summed up by one official letter:

'I acknowledge receipt of your complaint to the Security Service Tribunal which was received on 3 May 1990. The Security Service Act 1989 came into force on 18 December 1989 and is not *retrospective* [emphasis added]. You have stated in your complaint that the events to which you refer took place between January 1984 and November 1984 and they are not therefore within the *jurisdiction* of the tribunal. [emphasis added]

The Mind Controllers

I am sorry that I cannot be more helpful.
J.R. Harmer, Tribunal Secretary"[1]

Dargle Cottage is situated about a mile and a half south-east of the village of Biddenden in Kent. Being an old woodcutter's cottage dating back to the days of the Battle of Waterloo, it stands in an isolated and secluded position, surrounded by thick woods. The Verneys acquired the cottage in the spring of 1969 and used it as their weekend holiday home. When they retired in the summer of 1983, they decided to move from their London flat and make the cottage their permanent home. Throughout the year, they spent a considerable amount of their savings on improvements to the cottage, as well as furniture, to make the cottage comfortable for their retirement days.

Anthony Verney had been an inspector for The Good Food Guide for 25 years and he had also worked for the Consumers Association on the Good Hotel Guide. Both Mr Verney and his wife had been looking into expanding their interest in these fields during their retirement. For, as well as working in the consumer rights field, Mr Verney was also a founder of the Writer's Guild of Great Britain, and he enjoyed writing for theatre, film and television. He planned to return to his writing as his main pastime, and hoped to form a new company to market his work. As both of the Verneys had worked in theatre from an early age, they were anticipating an enjoyable time. Approximately three-quarters of a mile away, to the north-west of their cottage, was a 'timber yard' which manufactured gates and fences. In the years leading up to their retirement, there had been very little noise from the yard; all the couple would hear was the occasional staff call on the tannoy system. However, in early September 1983, the Verneys noticed a marked increase in machinery noise from the yard. They initially dismissed this as being a result of the firm's expansion, which meant that new water mains and drains were being installed.

Victims of Dargle Cottage

Mr Verney felt that the management was perhaps not taking the appropriate steps to minimise the increased noise levels, and decided to speak to the works manager, who showed some level of concern. However, his further approach to the managing director bore little result. He told Mr Verney that the firm had been in business since 1940 and that they were making no more noise than before. I should add that that part of Kent has had a large number of military establishments since 1940.

On 1 October 1983, while they were entertaining a visitor, the couple heard a mysterious noise. It was completely different to any noise that had ever come from the timber yard before. The noise was loud and humming, and it extended to the entire area of the back of their cottage. It seemed as if the noise was coming up from the ground from an area about twenty yards away, close to the woods. They reported that the noise seemed to penetrate every cell in their bodies and bones, and that it was unlike anything they had heard before.

The strange noise continued over the next four days and nights. What stood out to them as being unusual was that as soon as the noise started, all other sounds in the wood died almost immediately, as if all the wildlife in the area had left the area. Much later, the Verneys noticed that the birds did not return to nest the following spring. After four days, the Verneys were at their wits' end, and they decided to go away on a holiday on 5 October 1983, in the hope that the noise would have vanished by the time they returned. Little did they know that their troubles had only just started.

When they returned on 25th October 1983, they noticed a marked increase in the sound levels; it was all around their house and at times it even seemed as if it was coming from inside the cottage itself. They also found that there was an added element; in the early hours of each morning, the noise took on a throbbing and vibrating quality. And, as the Verneys later complained: 'The woods to the north-east were lit up by yellow and pink lights, which appeared to come up through the ground, lighting up the trees; a similar effect to a theatre cyclorama.'[2]

When they returned, they discovered that their drains from the kitchen sink had been blocked with lumps of broken asphalt, which had to be cleared by hand. They had no idea who might have done this or why. By the beginning of November 1983, the situation had worsened. Although the humming had decreased, it had been replaced with a powerful throbbing noise with a regular beat. It was accompanied by violent vibrations, which seemed to come through the ground, enveloping their cottage and the surrounding area, and the sound was at its loudest in the small hours of the morning.[3] At times, it felt as if someone was deliberately trying to torture them when they most needed to rest.

The noise got steadily worse during November that year and interfered with their sleep at nights. The couple feared that the sound (which was composed of low frequency vibrations) was becoming a health hazard, and might be affecting their central nervous systems. Supposing that it might be emanating from a water pump or other agricultural activity, they made enquiries with the local Water Board, but the authorities assured them that they had no facilities in the area that could make such a noise.

Each night, the Verneys went out in a desperate attempt to locate the source of the noise. This proved impossible as it appeared to move around. In the course of one of their night searches on 24 November, they encountered a police patrol at about 1am. The strange noises were loud enough to be heard by the two officers, who thought that it might be coming from Shorts Wood to the north-east. The policemen promised to report the matter and contact the Verneys if they could locate the source.

Victims of Dargle Cottage

On the afternoon of Saturday, November 26, Mr. Verney called in at their local police station in Tenterden, where he was interviewed by the station sergeant. He discovered the police patrol had not reported the problem. Verney filed a complaint in the desk book (which was recorded in pencil) but otherwise the station sergeant proved to be unhelpful. He was told it was not a police matter, and that he should contact the local Environmental Health Department. However, he says he was also told by the officer that, 'You won't get much help from them. They are bloody useless.'

The following day, Verney called the Environmental Health Department. Since none of the officers were in, he left his telephone number with a secretary to whom he explained the nature of the problem. Disappointed with not receiving a call from an Environmental Health Officer (EHO), by December 1, the couple decided to get away from the place and the problem for a short while. The level of electronic noise was becoming intolerable.

The Verneys returned to the cottage on 6 December 1983. There were no messages on their answer phone from the environment people. Mr Verney left further messages for the EHO, never receiving a reply. He also wrote to the Borough Treasurer's Department, complaining about the noise pollution and requesting a reduction in rates.

The Verneys made inquiries to the Planning Department of their local council to see if there was planning permission for a building or housing unit that could be the cause of the troubling noise. None of these inquiries bore any meaningful fruit. Instead the situation became worse still; life was rapidly becoming intolerable inside the house.

Other factors were adding their already difficult living conditions; their electricity supply started to fluctuate. The electricity levels would increase and decrease for no apparent reason and, being their main source of energy, they were sometimes unable to cook, or even turn their lights on. On other occasions the lights would go up and down in intensity – eerily at one-minute intervals.

The same electricity sub-station also supplied the timber yard. Mr Verney complained to Seeboard, the South East Electricity Board, explaining to Mr Green (the Chief Electrical Engineer) the nature of the problem and the trouble they were having. He mooted the possibility that some electrical instrument in the timber yard could be drawing off too much power. Green seemed concerned and promised to see to the problem immediately.

On 20 December 1983, at about 8am, the surrounding woods were full of Seeboard men carrying out work on the power lines. A task force of about eight workers and two vans spent several hours on the site. Green himself was in charge, and explained to Verney that they were 'putting more power into the lines.' However, he failed to explain what was causing the problem. The electricity supply was improved, although the lighting continued to fluctuate for several weeks afterwards.

Having heard nothing from the EHO, the Verneys were not prepared to spend the forthcoming Christmas holiday being battered by noise or vibrations. Verney decided to seek independent advice and contacted a firm of acoustic engineers in Maidstone.

A representative of the firm came to see them that evening, 20 December 1983. Despite the wind and rain, the acoustic expert obtained a very strong reading on his instrument, especially from the vibrations. The expert stated that the main source was within less than a mile radius of the house. He said that he would report his findings to the EHO.

Eventually, on December 21, at about 4.45pm, an EHO officer phoned Verney, who outlined the nature of the problem to him. Verney says the EHO was most unforthcoming and would promise neither to look into the matter, nor take any action under the Control of Pollution Act. What was more annoying was the EHO's outright rejection of the possibility of putting equipment in the cottage to measure the noise level. The EHO claimed not to have any suitable instruments. Despite Verney offering to obtain the instruments himself, the EHO rejected any assistance and moreover, seemed to consider it improper that Verney had offered in the first place.

Despite the EHO's rebuff, Mr Verney called the same officer again the very next day to ask for help before the Christmas holidays began. He met with the same cold response. In complete desperation, Verney decided to take control of the situation. He travelled to London to see if he could hire some instruments to record the noise levels.

As it was the run-up to Christmas, the electrical shops were open late, and he found one on Tottenham Court Road, which had highly sophisticated equipment. Verney explained what was happening to two members of staff. He was perturbed when they quickly exchanged glances, and one of them said: 'It sounds as if you are having trouble with the Ministry of Defence (MOD). You won't get anywhere with them.' Sensing Verney's anxiety, they introduced him to a colleague who, they said, was a leading electronic scientist – 'and just the man for you.' He was promised help after the Christmas holidays.

For the whole time that this had been going on, the Verneys had not thought for one moment that the noise might be anything more than ordinary noise pollution. Like any other citizen in similar circumstances, they had assumed that it would be a simple industrial noise that could be dealt with through their local government authorities. The last thing Verney had suspected was MOD involvement. But with this new possibility, the reluctance of the EHO to help along with the police's refusal to pursue the matter became clear. Additionally, Verney soon discovered that the

MOD is not subject to the Control of Pollution Act (or any related civil law for that matter.)[4]

The couple began to grow increasingly uneasy, and they wondered whether they might be under surveillance, and they began to suspect that there might be a tap on their phone. While carrying out searches of their district trying to locate the source, the Verneys' curiosity was aroused by a new house that had been built only two years earlier. It was situated on Gribble Bridge Lane, in a direct line through the woods with their own cottage. The house was described on planning documents as a farm, but there were no signs of any agricultural activity apart from some beehives.

The house was surrounded with high hedges and was somewhat curious in its construction. It was two storeys high, but there were no windows on the second floor or at the back of the house – only on each side. It reminded Mr Verney of the edifices built by the German Army on the Channel coast during the Second World War.

Thick, opaque floor-length net curtains blocked the view into the ground floor windows. It later emerged that these were made from a textile manufactured exclusively for the Property Services Agency of the Department of the Environment. This textile was used to protect high security buildings such as those owned by the Ministry of Defence and the Security Services. They were not the sort of curtains that one would expect to see in an agricultural dwelling, which was the designation that was given in the planning permission by Ashford Borough Council.

At the front of the building, to the right from the road, there was some kind of bunker with a large mushroom-shaped air vent. The bunker ran down the side of the house for some distance. Having made further enquiries, Verney discovered that the telephone number for the house was classified. He found out that there was a couple in their forties living there, and that there were Doberman dogs guarding the premises.

The low frequency transmission ran throughout Christmas Eve. Verney noted: 'The nights were awful, with lots of activity with the lights[5] in and around the house.' The Verneys could not get any sleep and were totally exhausted.

On Christmas morning, when the rest of the country was opening their presents, the Verneys set out on foot in desperation, trying to pinpoint the source of the noise. It was audible most of the time. But, like a will'o'the wisp, it still seemed to move around, as if lost in folds in the ground. It seemed to be located in an area north of Shorts Wood, and close to the Gribble Stream, in accordance with the fix that the electronics expert had made.

Verney's local authority had produced a leaflet entitled 'Taking Action On A Noise Situation' which covered pollution caused by noisy parties, radios, and barking dogs among other things. Under the legislation quoted there was alas, no provisions for the type of noise the Verneys were suffering. In any case, in order to take action they had to locate and identify those responsible. Further to the advice given by the Council, they nevertheless started a log detailing the times and the nature of the disturbances to their lives.

Due to the mental pressure, the Verneys decided they would eventually have to move out. On 29 December 1983, the couple made a firm offer for a new house at Streat in Sussex. Upon their return to their cottage the noise was still there: a loud humming as well as the thump of the low frequency. It continued all day.

The Verneys' log gives a detailed account of its effects on the couple from 26 December 1983 until 20 May 1984: 'LOG BOOK – DARGLE COTTAGE, BOXING DAY, 26/12/1983

'The noise and vibrations went on at a high level all through the night. Sleep was impossible. The noise peaked at 4.15am, vibrations and a loud humming with a metallic note. The sound was recorded.[6]

'At first light there was a new feature. Horseshoe shaped lights moved across the sky from west to east, low against the background of the trees. The objects were lit up, like flying tiaras. They were three in number. They disappeared, losing height over the Shorts Wood – Gribble Wood area.

'27/12/1983

'Impossible to get much sleep in the early hours. A big escalation at 3.50am in noise and vibrations, and a loud humming. Activity with light goes on and off [flying tiaras]. At 5.45am the noise and vibrations increased still more and with a faster beat. The flying tiaras appeared again, flying from west to east as before.'

Not having had any rest, the Verneys decided to leave their cottage and seek refuge at the Halland Motel in East Sussex. They had begun to believe that the low frequency transmissions were in fact pouring radiation into their home. Neither the police nor the council were willing to take any action. On 18 January 1984, according to an arrangement they had made earlier, Mr Verney drove to Wapping to pick up Mr D., the electronics expert that he had met in London before Christmas. They stopped off for lunch at the Three Chimneys Public House, but while they were eating, his car was broken into, his cheque book and January bank statement (outlining expenditure in the month of December) were stolen. When they arrived at the cottage, there was – unusually – no noise that could be heard. Ten minutes later, the EHO suddenly appeared. Verney had not told them about the arrangement to bring the scientist back, but the council official seemed agitated, and moreover, he knew Mr D's name. 'So – you are Mr D,' he said. The sight of the equipment the official extremely uneasy. 'What is going on here?' he asked. He then proceeded to cross-examine Mr D on what he was going to do and where he came from. His behaviour was more like a police interrogator than a local authority employee. He then returned the tape recordings of the noise Mr Verney had made without making any comments about them.

Mr. D was suspicious about a bandage on the EHO's finger, which extended some way beyond the end of the digit; he worried that it hid some form of two-way radio. Major Fred Holroyd, a former intelligence officer in Northern Ireland, has said he was in possession of a unit of this kind when serving in Ulster – and that it was supplied to him by the SAS. Such an instrument would have been in possession of the Joint Intelligence Training Unit at Ashford, Kent, in 1984. On the way back to his car, the EHO commented that he could hear no noise. However, just as he said this there was a sudden, intense flurry of sound, and he cried, 'I have never heard *that* so loud.'

Mr D came out to lower a rifle-microphone into the well outside the front of the house, to see what he could pick up. In response to Mr D's invitation to stay and see the results, the EHO said he had seen and heard what he had come for, and left. There was a high positive reading of vibrations inside the well, which must have been propagated through the ground.

Mr Verney was convinced that the only way the EHO could have known the name, and time of arrival of the scientist, was by their phone being tapped, or some other means of eavesdropping.

Mr D stayed for seven hours, during which time, the noise level mysteriously abated. Mr Verney took him back to London, leaving Doreen Verney on her own. This was a mistake, as not long after their departure, the noise and vibrations began again. It was as though they were being watched. Mrs Verney said the next day that she had had the most terrible night yet. She claims that as a result of that night, her hair turned white within forty-eight hours. At the end of his tether, Mr Verney rang the EHO once more. Yet again, his cries for help fell on deaf ears. By now, it was clear that the source of the noise and vibrations was under the ground. When Mr. Verney had played one of his recordings to a caller from the 'Agricultural Dwelling' department in the council, the lady listener was shocked and alarmed. 'Oh,' she cried, 'is it THAT bad?' She then promised to help to find the culprits. But as soon as Verney said he suspected the source to be an underground installation less than a mile from their cottage, she hung up and they never heard from her again.

On 21 March 1984, the couple put the cottage on the market for sale. The Verneys spent as little time as they could in the house – no more than two nights at a time – and in April they found a prospective buyer. On 5 April 1984, they received a call at their London flat from a Detective Constable George Keeler of Ashford CID, to the effect that a window had been broken at their home in Kent, but that no-one had apparently broken in.

On returning they found the hall was full of splinters, and there were white paint particles from the door in the hall leading into the main part of the house. It had been kicked in and the mortice lock was left hanging. The intruders had exited by a stable-type door at the rear.

The matter was reported to Tenterden Police Station. DC Keeler was somewhat uneasy to hear that despite his earlier report to the Verneys, the place had in fact been entered. It was obvious the police had not made a proper check.

What was peculiar was that nothing of value was stolen, except Mr Verney's private papers relating to his tax, some private letters of a personal nature from a Privy Counsellor and former Cabinet Minister, a friend of the family of many years standing, and part of a bar of Bournville chocolate. Someone had gone through his desk in the study and had checked the contents of his files. Keeler said sarcastically, 'I suppose I better look for someone with chocolate on their teeth.'

The Verneys spent seven nights in May in the cottage. Despite some very bad nights of noise, it was not as extreme as before. On May 18, their daughter Eugenie and a friend came to spend the weekend. They helped the Verneys to pack because they were to move out shortly. That night, Mr Verney woke up with an intense burning sensation in his eyes. It was extremely painful and continued until 7am.

Eugenie Verney said that she was terrified out of her wits and that she had heard men shouting in the woods. She says that for a week after staying at the cottage she suffered serious loss of memory and was off work. On their way back home, her friend was taken ill on the M1. Fortunately, he was able to pull off the road at a nearby service station, where he passed out.

But the worst was still yet to come. At about 1.30am on 20 May 1984, all hell was let loose at Dargle cottage. The noise was at its highest level yet heard. The vibrations tore through the ground of the woods and towards the house, and the vibrations were at a frightening level; literally shaking the building in its foundations. Similar kinds of bangs to those heard previously came from the woods until after 7am.

Anthony and Doreen Verney were totally shattered and feeling extremely ill. They had to abandon the house once more. They moved out on the morning of 23 May 1984 with Doreen in great pain, hardly able to walk.

Mrs Verney was later confined to an old people's rest home. She had aged tremendously due to the torment she had been put through. Mr Verney was also old and frail, but remained brave and bold. For a man who had fought the Nazis, it seemed his country had failed him. The question remained: what was causing the noise?

The Mind Controllers

Footnotes

1. Letter dated 3 May 1990, from the Security Service Tribunal to Mr. A.R. Verney.

2. Telephone conversation between the author and Mr. Verney, also his notes entitled 'The Happy Retirement'. [copy enclosed]

3. Mr Verney provided the author with copies of the noise tape recorded at various dates throughout their ordeal. The noise is identical to another tape provided to the author by Mr. Joe Vialls (another victim) whose account is documented in 'Open Verdict'; Tony Collins, Sphere Books Ltd., 1990. Dr Robert Becker, a world authority on microwaves, has examined Mr. Verney's tapes. Dr Becker has been a candidate for the Nobel Prize in Physics, and his books (Cross Current and Body Electric) provide an in depth and peer account on the biological effects of microwaves. The author has also had several conversations with Dr Becker concerning these tapes and the status of the current technologies available to the military today.

4. This seems to be the case. Several residents in Wales and North Yorkshire have been continuously complaining about the noise of low flying RAF fighter aircraft on residential areas without much success.

5. See note 2.

6. See note 3.

Chapter Eight

Passing the Buck

One report from US files may have a bearing on the Verneys' plight: 'A decoy and deception concept presently being considered is to remotely create the perception of noise in the heads of personnel by exposing them to low power, pulsed microwaves. When people are illuminated with properly modulated low power microwaves the sensation is reported as a buzzing, clocking, or hissing which seems to originate (regardless of the person's position in the field) within or just behind the head. The phenomenon occurs at average power densities as low as microwatts per square centimetre with carrier frequencies from 0.4 to 3.0 Ghz. By proper choice of pulse characteristics, intelligible speech may be created. Before this technique may be extended and used for military applications, an understanding of the basic principles must be developed. Such an understanding is not only required to optimize the use of the concept for camouflage, decoy and deception operations but is required to properly assess safety factors of such microwave exposure. Oscar, Kenneth J. US Army Mobility Equipment Research and Development Command – Fort Belvoir, VA'

Mr and Mrs Verney believed they were subjected to an array of hazardous non-ionising irradiation, Very Low Frequency (VLF) pulses, over a considerable period of time. They also believe they were attacked on about eight occasions by an electromagnetic pulse, which must have been deliberately deployed against them.

The effects of VLF on the human system have been well documented. Both VLF and ELF (extremely low frequency) are non-ionising radiation, which causes serious disturbance in the blood cells. VLF in particular attacks the lower nervous system and effects the lower half of the body, the lumbar region, as well as the lower part of the spine, thighs and upper legs. It causes serious disorientation, headaches and ringing in the ears. Depression and irritability are other side effects, plus the loss of memory.

When the Verneys left Dargle Cottage at the end of January 1984, they drove to Scotland. They felt they were so saturated with radiation that they had become sensitised to it.

Mr Verney said his body 'could pick up' on a generator over a mile away. 'It is a very strange sensation; at times the body feels as if it is on fire.'

Doreen said she could detect electrical junction boxes over quarter of a mile away. She had a ringing in her ears for over ten days afterwards. This increased at times when she was in the vicinity of an electrical transmission.

She said that electromagnetic pulses caused an excruciating headache, as if an electrical drill was boring into it. She would bury her head under bedclothes but the effects were even worse – because when there was no noise, it caused complete disorientation.

In January and February 1984, Mrs Doreen Verney suffered two attacks of severe stomach cramps, accompanied by vomiting. This is usually the first indication of the effects of radiation, which is described as such in the manuals issued to the Armed Forces by the MOD. She was ill throughout March, and in early April her GP sent her to be examined by a specialist in cancer. Various tests failed to uncover anything serious.

Following the attack on Dargle Cottage on 20 May 1984, she became more seriously ill. On the morning of 23 May 1984, when they moved out, she had severe pain in her legs and lumbar region, and she was almost unable to walk. Further medical tests once more failed to reveal the cause.

She then began to suffer from attacks of diarrhoea. Her health continued to deteriorate during June and July 1984 and she put on a great deal of weight around the waist – formerly she had been a very fit and slim person. Further blood tests, X-rays and body scans revealed nothing. However, a third body scan on 24 August 1984 showed a large area of fluid on the left side of her chest.

On 31 August 1984, she was admitted to the Fitzroy Nuffield Hospital in London, where five and half pints of infected fluid was drawn off her chest. She was diagnosed as suffering from a rare and dangerous form of lymphatic leukaemia and went into surgery on the morning of 1 September 1984. Doctors gave her only a 10% chance of survival. With two months of chemotherapy, she pulled through. However, Doreen had become a semi-invalid; a person who had been so full of life and had been looking forward to a happy retirement could hardly walk, and suffered much pain.

Her husband was severely ill for three weeks from the end of February until middle of March 1984. He also suffered from acute pains in the back, lumbar region and thighs. He had difficulty walking, or even staying upright, and he found it hard to keep his balance. His continuous pain also prevented him from proper sleep or rest.

Medical tests in March revealed that his metabolism was very disturbed, and that his blood cells were severely affected. His blood sedimentation level, which had been normal at 8 per cent had shot up to 30 per cent. Anything above this level is considered extremely serious.

The events of 20 May 1984, made matters even worse. Over the years he had taken very good care of his teeth, making regular visits to a Harley Street dental surgeon. Over the three months between March and May, he lost most of his teeth. Some fell out and others simply crumbled. This is a well-known symptom of ionising radiation, and a feature amongst servicemen who took part in the atomic tests in Australia during the 1950s. X-rays also revealed permanent damage to his lower lumber region and spinal cord.

For over three years he suffered from a problem with his macrocytes, and a continual over-production of red blood cells. This is a condition described as polythemia, discovered in US servicemen exposed to electromagnetic pulses.

He had also suffered from three severe attacks of something akin to shingles but uncharacteristically it recurred in the same places. It also lasted longer than shingles would, and the spots left scars which did not fade. He also suffered from pains in his limbs, and a recurring problem of frequent painful enlargement of the nipples.

Sometime later, in July 1989 and January 1990, Anthony Verney underwent two operations in the Wellington Day Centre and the Hassocks Health Centre. On the first occasion it was for the removal of suspected basal carcinoma, the second time for removal of lesions. On both occasions the doctors (Dr D. Dowling Munro, and Dr Lucy Free) were unable to identify the cause and nature of his complaint. According to US Navy Surface Weapons Center studies on the effects of microwave weapons, it has been established that hot spots in the brain, lesions and necrosis of internal tissues can be induced. They can also affect heart function.

Prior to their problems, in June 1983, Mr and Mrs Verney both had full medical examinations at the Tenterden Health Centre, in connection with a pension scheme with Allied Hambro (now Allied Dunbar). Both came through the tests very well, as the records show.

Mr Verney provided me with a complete list of doctors and surgeons who treated him and his wife during their ordeal. I spoke to Dr Douglas Rossdale, their General Practitioner on 28 March 1991, and asked him his opinion on the case. Dr Rossdale paid tribute to the Verneys, and their resilience in spite of the difficulties they had been through. He added that in the many years he had been in practice, the couple's case was unique.

Both patients suffered from a similar and unusual syndrome simultaneously – a situation relatively rare in medical practice. He was also surprised by the rapid deterioration of their health, and taking into consideration their previous medical history, he could not identify the cause.

There is little doubt that the police could have taken action, tracked down the source of the noise, found the culprits and prosecuted as a breach of the peace. But for some unexplained reason they chose not to. What is ironic, however, is that a few months later during the Coal Miner's dispute, the Kent Police took extraordinary steps to interfere with the movement of vehicles suspected of carrying striking miners out of the county, alleging that they were threatening a breach of the peace.

Anthony Verney wrote to the Chancellor of Exchequer (at that time Nigel Lawson) complaining about their ordeal and claiming compensation. In February 1986, he received a postcard from George Younger, then Private Secretary of Defence. This was followed by a letter from Mr S.M. Murray, a Senior Claims Officer at the Ministry of Defence.

Murray stated in his letter that what had happened to the Verneys had nothing to do with the Ministry of Defence (this had apparently been the view of Lawson's office as well). 'But,' he added, 'it was due to the activities of criminal elements in the area and a matter for the *civil police*' [emphasis added].

After almost three years, Anthony Verney at last thought he had obtained a legitimate response, which might force the police to take the long overdue action. A copy of this missive was sent to the Chief Constable of the Kent Constabulary. After several reminders and a long period of waiting he received an acknowledgement.

In the first week of March 1987 (over a year since his correspondence with Nigel Lawson) he received a call from an Inspector Watkins of the Kent Police, requesting an appointment to discuss the matter. Two weeks later the inspector and a colleague arrived for a 90 minute discussion. Watkins disclosed he had already called on Murray in his office at the MOD asking him to support his statement concerning 'criminal elements in the area' with evidence. Murray had proved to be non-committal, informing the police there were 'no military establishments in the Biddenden area', something the local police already knew.

The two visiting officers were horrified by the recordings made at Dargle Cottage. They were in agreement with Verney that the operation at Biddenden was probably the work of some units involving scientists or MOD contractors, who did not come under the direct control of the Ministry of Defence, but were conducting trials and experiments on the MOD's behalf.

The police officers were particularly angry about the failure of the local authority to enforce the Control of Pollution Act, 1974, about which they seemed well-briefed. They particularly singled out the Medical Officer for Health for the Ashford area as being negligent in his duties. At the end of the meeting, Mr Verney asked Inspector Watkins for his opinion. He replied that it 'was due to the activities of an organisation over whom they, (the Kent Police), had no jurisdiction.'

Subsequently, Verney tried to obtain a written confirmation of Inspector Watkins statement. On 5 August 1987, he received a letter from the Deputy Constable of Kent County Constabulary. It stated: 'I refer to your letter dated the 30th July, 1987, concerning the visit of Inspector Watkins to you earlier this year. Your comments have been noted. The issues initially raised in your letter are not matters which fall within the jurisdiction of the Kent Police. Additional enquiries by this Force are unlikely to assist you in your claims against Ashford Borough Council, or the Treasury. Under the circumstances I must reluctantly inform you that no further action will be taken and no other correspondence will be entered into in respect of these matters.'

It was obvious that the Kent Police did not wish to make any further inquiries into the case, as with the break-in. It is equally obvious that to implement the Control of Pollution Act, 1974, which the local council should have enforced, the necessary test equipment could have been found – either rented, or borrowed from the Health and Safety Executive, various scientific institutions or Kent or Sussex universities. Southampton University has a Noise & Vibration Unit.

The Medical Health Officer (MHO) also refused to take any action. According to Verney: 'Callous disregard was the flavour of all correspondence from the Council.'

As noted above, the noise and vibration was sometimes accompanied by unusual lights in the sky, or 'flying tiaras', as Verney described them. Others saw them as well; Councillor Hawksley of Ashford Borough Council stated that she had seen pink lights in that area on more than one occasion. The EHO volunteered the information of sightings reported by members of the public who called them UFOs in the area.

Over the years, Verney conducted a sporadic correspondence with Eddie Mexter, the Chief Executive of the Ashford Borough Council, regarding the EHO's strange behaviour and his failure to enforce the law. Mexter, distancing himself from his own subordinates in January 1989, advised Verney he could have taken independent legal action 'against those responsible' for inaction. It was surprising advice from the Chief Executive, a solicitor, in a matter concerning a department that was under his jurisdiction.

On 25 March 1988, Tim Rathbone, Verney's Member of Parliament, addressed his serious concerns to Margaret Thatcher, the Prime Minister. In her reply of

12 May 1988, she acknowledged that Verney had had numerous correspondence 'with various Ministers and Government Departments since February 1986 alleging that he and his wife had been subjected to 'electronic pollution and radiation' at their former home in Kent between October 1983 and May 1984.'[1] She went on to add that: 'It was suggested that the nature of the incidents described seemed to suggest criminal activities by persons unknown, rather than the legitimate activities of servants or agents of the Crown, and so it might be more appropriate for him to pursue the matter with the Civil Police authorities.'[2]

Lord Denning, former Master of the Rolls, gave some sage advice to Verney at the same time. To bring the culprits to book you first have to find them and it they are government agents that was a major difficulty.' They operate so secretly that they have come and gone before you can know.'[3]

Through another MP, Merlyn Rees, the matter was raised with John Major, the Prime Minister, in 1992. The reply was predictable: 'I am afraid there is nothing I can usefully add to this (previous) correspondence, and I can only repeat that Mr Verney's allegations are considered to be totally unfounded.'[4]

In February 1992, Phil Chamberlin, from University of Sussex Students Union took up Verney's case, and corresponded with Robin Corbett MP, enclosing a copy of Verney's file. Corbett replied; 'I was so disturbed about the aspects of the file that I asked a Privy Counsellor friend of mine to send it to the Prime Minister, which he has done.'[5] No useful response was obtained.

In a letter to Amnesty International on 15 January 1992, I sought their assistance in analysing Verney's tapes.[6]

On 14 February 1992, Jane Dykins, MSP Working Group Volunteer, Amnesty International informed me; 'We have no information on audio tapes, or whether there are any means to analyse the taped content.'[7]

On 6 May 1992, Major reiterated the need for secrecy about intelligence service operations. He told Parliament: 'The Government has deliberately distinguished between publicly acknowledging the existence of both of the Security Service and the Secret Intelligence Service and commenting on operational information. That it is a distinction which the Government will continue to maintain.'[8]

But the battle went on. In March 1996, Justin Williams, a journalist from the Kent Messenger Newspapers Group became involved in Verneys' case. After contacting me, Williams tried to establish what had happened, and later on 26 April 1996, he published an account of his findings in his paper.[9] He too was somewhat surprised by his findings, and the way he was treated by the witnesses in the course of his investigation. In his letter of 21 May 1996, Justin wrote to me: 'In the case of Verney, I, like you, am convinced that he fell victim to something. What to me is more likely is that something covert was going on in Short Wood, possibly directed from October Farm, that the British military establishment had knowledge of but were not directly involved in.

'It is still unclear what happened to Verneys, or why. Latterly Verney became convinced that he had been targeted for some reason, but I thought it more likely he and his wife were unfortunate enough to have been in the way of something – accidental victims of some experiment. It says a great deal about this benighted country, and the sheer stupidity of so many of its secret servants that rather than just admit this, apologise, and offer restitution, the British state went into full scale cover-up and harassment mode.'[10]

Doreen Verney died in March 1996. A few months later in September, Anthony Verney passed away. He had checked himself into a psycho-geriatric ward against the advice of family and friends, apparently in the hope that he would get relief from what he still perceived as microwave pollution

The Mind Controllers

Footnotes

1. Margaret Thatcher (PM) letter of 12 May 1988.

2. ibid.

3. Lord Denning letter of 30 January 1988.

4. John Major (PM) letter of 20 February 1992.

5. Robin Corbett MP letter of 10 February 1992.

6. Robin Corbett MP letter of 26 February 1992.

7. Amnesty International letter of 14 February 1992.

8. Simon Watkin (Home Office) letter of 2 October 1992.

9. Short Wood Mystery, Kent Messenger, 26 April 1996.

10. Lobster, December 1996, Obituaries column.

Chapter Nine

Psychic Research

Those who do not believe in the existence of anything non-physical, such as mind, soul, spirit, until they have good evidence that they exist, should also not believe in extrasensory perception (ESP). ESP refers to the human acquisition of information about the future, past, or present, without using the five known senses.

The term was coined for the first time by J.B. Rhine, one-time head of the world's first university parapsychology department. Rhine set up the Foundation for Research into the Nature of Man (FRNM) with an Institute for Parapsychology off-campus in Durham, NC, where it remained after his death in 1980. ESP encompasses the use of telepathy, clairvoyance, and precognition as follows:

(1) Telepathy addresses the transmission of information from one mind to another without the use of language, body language, or any known senses.

(2) Clairvoyance pertains to the acquisition of information not previously known to the recipient by any known senses. Even more significant is that the nature and the contents of the information received is not known to anyone apart from the recipient – for example if one could read pages of a closed book, or identify the contents in a closed box.

(3) Precognition is the acquisition of information about an event before it takes place.

Although there is abundant anecdotal evidence regarding the existence of ESP, science to date has chosen to pay little attention to its study. Nevertheless, military and intelligence communities around the world have granted ESP significant importance in terms of its exploitation both offensively and defensively.

The Mind Controllers

On 27 August 1995, the British Channel Four television programme 'The Real X-Files' gave a glimpse of the long history of US psychic research programmes (psi). As most of these programmes have been 'black' (or secret), results have been concealed from the public and Congress. The triggering mechanism for the Pentagon's intense interest in this field (funded through the Central Intelligence Agency, with the help and association of DIA, NSA, as well as a number of governmental and non-governmental research laboratories) has been the substantial progress made by the former Soviet Union, and her satellites.

From the records in hand it is clear that until around 1970 the US government had taken little notice of psychic research and its possible implications for intelligence and warfare. The CIA had investigated the use of psi for intelligence gathering purposes in the early fifties, but in the rather ad hoc way police departments sometimes seek assistance from psychics to solve a crime.[1] In the course of their famous mind control projects code-named ARTICHOKE, BLUEBIRD and MKULTRA, the CIA allocated a small portion of the budget to study the use of mediums in seeking intelligence from the dead, and called for a scientific study of the use of psychics for intelligence work.[2]

In the early sixties, the US Air Force commissioned the American Institute for Research [AIR] to conduct a feasibility study in the development and use of psychological phenomena for warfare. AIR published their findings under the title of 'Psychological Phenomena Applicable To The Development of Psychological Weapons' in December 1965.[3] In their report, AIR stressed the possibilities, including the use of lasers, electromagnetic frequencies and sound. These techniques are currently under serious development, some under the so-called new concept of 'non-lethal weapons'.[4]

Dr J. G. Pratt of the Department of Psychiatry at the University of Virginia was one of the first researchers from the West to visit the Soviet Union following the publication of the work of their expert, Leonid Vasiliev.[5] He described how the atmosphere of meetings arranged by Dr Eduard Naumov changed between 1963 and 1968. During the first visit, the conference was open, cordial and ripe for the exchange of information. But on his 1968 visit there were clear signs of unease.

By then, the Soviet official organ 'Pravda' had published an article attacking parapsychology. Most of the Soviet scientists declined to deliver their research papers and Western visitors were pressed to give impromptu lectures, and after this visit, the conference organisers withdrew their invitations to the West to hold further meetings or to allow films to be shown.[6]

The publication of 'Psychic Discoveries Behind the Iron Curtain' in 1970 raised public interest about mind control in the USA.[7] This publication, along with subsequent broadcasts made by the Voice of America to the Soviet Union on the subject of mind control made the climate in the Soviet Union worse still.[8]

In 1973, four eminent members of the Moscow Academy of Sciences published a lengthy paper, 'Parapsychology, Fiction or Reality?' in 'Questions of Philosophy', an official publication of the Soviet Academy of Pedagogical Sciences. It attacked parapsychology and its researchers. This change of line was further illustrated in 1974 when the Soviet parapsychologist Edward Naumov, mentioned above, who was the key Soviet contact for the authors of 'Psychic Discoveries Behind the Iron Curtain', was sentenced to two years hard labour for a petty offence and remanded to a psychiatric 'treatment facility'.[9] The change in the official line seems to have been an attempt not only to bar Western researchers from Soviet work but also to convince the USA that such work was not being seriously pursued in the Soviet Union.[10]

But by 1970, US intelligence had become seriously

interested in Soviet research into parapsychology.
Before 1971, when the American Intelligence community began investigating their Cold War enemy's work,
the CIA had conducted cursory investigations.[11] The
CIA discovered that the Soviets were spending approximately 60 million roubles per year in psychic
research. (The Soviets used a Czech neologism,
psychotronics, to describe their research.) By 1975,
this sum had increased to 300 million roubles – not a
trivial sum to spend on researching a controversial
subject.[12]

It was not so much the Soviet research which raised
CIA's concern, but its operational applications. It was
obvious that the Soviet's tight security control, which
prevented any information leakage, meant that they
must have had some serious breakthrough.

CIA analysts were faced with a dilemma. They were
uneasy about explaining to the main scientific advisors
of the National Security Council (NSC) that both the
KGB and GRU (Soviet Military Intelligence) were
researching topics considered in US to be speculative
and controversial at best. On the other hand, they
were afraid that the Soviets might win the psychotronic race, as they had done with the Sputnik.[13]

Finally, they came up with a solution. By coining the
phrase 'Psychic Warfare Gap', they convinced the NSC
to take action. By then the US intelligence community
was aware that psychotronics had an application, and
that something psychically aggressive might threaten
the security of the US. With Congressional approval,
they set out to research and examine the nature of this
threat.[14]

The CIA adopted a twin-track approach. Publicly,
through continuous disinformation campaigns, they
endeavoured to discredit psychic research. But secretly, they funded a series of projects and programmes
over a sixteen year period, on which they spent over
$20 million.[15] The Soviets, aware of the US activity,
reacted similarly. They too publicly denied the credi-

bility of any psychic research, imprisoned a number of researchers, particularly those involved in information exchange with their Western counterparts, and closed down several research institutes engaged in psychic research.

Soviet attempts to train their cosmonauts in telepathy initially aroused the CIA's attention. Their attempts were tested in March 1967, when a coded telepathic message was flashed from Moscow to Leningrad.[16] Four years later, Edgar Mitchell made a similar attempt in the course of his flight with the Apollo 14. Mitchell's attempt was based on studies and findings of four years of research and study, funded by the CIA, which started in 1970 in Maimonides Hospital in Brooklyn.

Among projects cited, there was study of telepathy-in-dreams, by the Dream Laboratory of the Maimonides Medical Center. Their studies suggested that dreams may be influenced telepathically, with images or concepts transmitted from an individual in a waking state to one who is dreaming.[17] The Soviets were pursuing the same goals.

In 1970, Maimonides Directors Stanley Kripner and Montague Ulman had presented one such controlled study with astonishingly positive results.[18] Fifteen follow-up studies provided similar results. As Maimonides' findings began to converge with the CIA's intelligence on the Soviet Union's research, the military applications and implications became more coherent. As before, the CIA had concealed its funding by diverting it through the McDonnell Aerospace Foundation.[19] Jack Houck, an aerospace engineer interested in the subject, was McDonnell's contact in the experiments. The National Institute of Health provided the other half of the funding. CIA funding of this research continued until 1982.

Shawn Robbins, a psychic participating in the dream studies, had provided good results and shortly afterwards he was contacted by the Office of Naval Intelligence [ONI]. The US Navy was interested in testing his psychic abilities on Soviet naval targets.[20] Robbins was provided with charts and photographs of Soviet ships, and was asked, after locating them, to predict their destinations.

The Parapsychological Association Convention of 1973, in Charlottesville, Virginia, provided more evidence that the Soviet line of research was well worth pursuing. Pratt and Keil, two American researchers recently returned from the USSR, reported their findings and observations of the Soviet psychic Kulagina.[21] Montague Ulman, Director of Maimonides Community Mental Health Center, Brooklyn, also gave a presentation on Kulagina. Charles Honorton described the results of psychokinetic studies he had conducted in Maimonides.[22]

Parallel research was on going at the Stanford Research Institute (SRI). SRI used fully awake subjects in their studies and experiments – though the procedures were almost identical to Maimonides. SRI was supported by the Navy and the CIA. (Later NASA also played a small role.[23]) There are clear indications of collaboration between Drs Puthoff and Targ from the SRI, and Edwin C. May, a consultant to SRI and a research associate in Division of Parapsychology and Psychophysics at Maimonides.[24]

SRI, too, followed the Soviet research line and duplicated experiments. An example was the work of Nikolaiev and Kamensky who showed that when a sender was exposed to a rapidly flashing light, the EEG of the receiver showed driving – i.e. telepathic influence – by the sender.[25]

SRI had termed their telepathy work Remote Viewing (RV). It was coined at a gathering on 8 December 1971 by Ingo Swann, a homosexual New York artist,[26] Dr Janet Mitchell, Dr Karlis Osis, and Dr Gertrude Schmeidler at the American Society for Psychical Research (ASPR), in New York City. In the course of their ten 'out-of-body perceptual state' experiments, ASPR attempted to locate hidden items on their premises using clairvoyant perception. They succeeded.

ASPR later decided to expand these experiments to targets outside their premises. Upon Swann's suggestion, Dr Janet Mitchell would give him the name of an American city. Swann would attempt to determine the weather condition there. Dr Mitchell would then telephone the local weather bureau to see if Swann was correct.

Ingo Swann's 1971 experiments were based on earlier, similar work conducted by French researcher, René Warcolier (1881-1962) who, during the 1920's, had conducted similar long-distance experiments between Paris and New York,[27] and J. Hittinger, a British researcher.[28]

Between the terms 'remote viewing' and 'remote sensing' Swann argued the latter is more apt, but Drs Osis and Schmeidler preferred 'remote viewing'.[29]

Swann took these experiments a step further. A person would go 'outbound' as a 'beacon' to a distant site somewhere in Manhattan. At a prearranged time this beacon made notes on the site – whilst his location would remain unknown to Swann in ASPR premises. Swann would then focus on the beacon, attempting to describe where he was.[30] The first of these experiments took place on 22 February 1972.[31]

In her book 'Out of Body Experiences', Dr Janet Mitchell suggests that these experiments were designed to ascertain 'whether a person could localise part of his or her consciousness in space some distance from the body.'[32] Mitchell believes the targets in these experiments might have been perceived telepathically, clairvoyantly, precognitively, or fraudulently. Ingo Swann suggests that 'they were perceived by some type of perception which operated outside of normal visual range.'[33]

Swann extrapolates further: 'We are talking about whether the bio-human possesses additional receptors for organising information that exceeds the local limits of the five physical senses. This he does with the help of at least seventeen more different types of senses that have been identified by biologists and neurologists.'[34] At SRI the remote viewing tests involved a receiver, writing any impressions noted from a sender – almost parallel with the Maimonides experiments, but with one difference. In SRI experiments the receiver was awake.[35] To prevent cheating, targets were randomly selected and the destinations only removed from a sealed envelope by the sender, after the sender and the team were en-route to the target area.

The sender remained in the target area for a designated time, while the receiver – the remote viewer – recorded his or her received impressions. The CIA's main contact in funding SRI's work was Harold Chipman. The US Navy's Project Manager in SRI was James Foote.[36]

Another important figure at that time was Andrija Puharich. Born in Chicago in 1918 of Yugoslav parents, Puharich was a medical doctor with a Ph.D. in physics. His military connections dated back to the 1950s when he worked in the Army's Chemical and Biological Warfare Center at Fort Detrick, Maryland. In 1952, he presented a paper, 'An Evaluation of the Possible Uses of Extrasensory Perception in Psychological Warfare', to a secret Pentagon gathering. In 1953, he lectured the US Air Force researchers on methods of increasing or decreasing telepathy, and the US Army Chemical Center on 'Biological Foundations of Extrasensory Perception'.

He mostly worked on follow-up studies of Soviet experiments; in 1962, he published an account of his studies based on his participation in programmes carried out in the 1950s.[37] He described biological explanations and hypothetical possibilities for psi and also underlined the effects of drugs, which were consistent with the CIA's mind control programmes and findings of that era.[38]

Puharich had a keen interest in parapsychology. In

1956, he brought Peter Horkus, a Dutch psychic, to the US, to help police in solving crime,[39] and, with the aid of the US astronaut Edgar Mitchell, he brought Uri Geller to SRI in 1972.

Throughout his career, the CIA was interested in Puharich, partly due to the fact his previous research findings were in line with the CIA's work in mind control, and partly due to Uri Geller's participation in psychic research experiments. Mossad had provided SRI with an intelligence report on Geller's abilities.[40] At SRI the most notable subjects were Ingo Swann, Patrick Price and Uri Geller; the important projects were SCANATE [CIA-NSA]; and Grill Flame [DIA], which will be examined in more depth in the next chapter.[41]

ASPR experiments, using a 'beacon', were not of much use for any espionage remote viewing programme: they required an agent to be placed in the target area, which was not feasible operationally. And providing the name of the distant target would have resulted in too much cueing of the viewer. Swann consulted with a number of scientists outside SRI circles in Silicon Valley, on how to combat this problem. Eventually, Jacques Vallée came up with a solution. He suggested that Swann use an address as the focus. Swann later developed this into map co-ordinates – latitude and longitude – leading to the birth of Project SCANATE.

SCANATE [SCANing by co-ordinATE] started on 29 May 1973, and was completed in 1975. It sent a chilling message to the military and intelligence chiefs. When Ingo Swann made his first attempt at remote viewing a site having only been given his co-ordinates, he had startling results. He described the features of the small French administered island of Kerguelen in the Southern Indian Ocean, including the layout of buildings and what appeared to be a joint French-Soviet meteorological research installation. He even drew a passable map of the island.

Later, using co-ordinates supplied by a sceptical

colleague on the East Coast, Swann described and drew a site that he felt might be some sort of military installation. Weeks later, the East Coast colleague confirmed that Swann's descriptions were correct in every detail.[42] Swann comments: 'It was to be nearly six years before I saw a topographical map of Kerguelen, which included the buildings and other man-made features. I had missed some of them, but was told that the major buildings were orange and there were a number of outhouses whose locations needed to be moved every once in a while.' The Kerguelen experiment was not classified, and, about a week later, the intelligence community leaked the details.

Pat Price gave an equally detailed account of a site. Harold Puthoff gave Price a set of map co-ordinates for the target in a very special remote viewing experiment. The co-ordinates described an area roughly 135 miles south-west of Washington, DC. Price's response surprised Puthoff. In a five page running commentary of his remote viewing tour, Price started off 1500 feet above the site and went through a complex of buildings and underground storage areas. The report described communication and computer equipment manned by Army Signal Corps personnel, names on desks in the building and even the labels on file folders in a locked cabinet in one of the rooms.[43] He quoted code words such as Flytrap, Minerva, Operation Pool; and folders labelled Cueball, 14 Ball, 4 Ball, 8 Ball, Rackup. He also named the site – Haystack – and the personnel stationed there; Col. R.J. Hamilton, Major General George R. Nash, and Major John C. Calhoun. A security officer present stated, 'Hell there's no security left.'

The Executive Summary of the CIA Final Report of the second year, provides an insight into Pat Price and Ingo Swann's coordinated RV work funded by the CIA: 'In order to subject the remote viewing phenomena to a rigorous long-distance control, a request for geographical coordinates of a site unknown to subject and experimenters was forwarded to the [CIA's] OSI [Office of Scientific Intelligence] group responsible for threat analysis in this area. In response SRI personnel received a set of facility [co-ordinates] hereafter referred to as the West Virginia Site. The experimenters then carried out a remote viewing experiment on a double-blind basis, that is blind to experimenters as well as subject. The experiment had as its goal the determination of the utility of remote viewing under conditions approximating an operational scenario. Two subjects [were] targeted on the site, a sensitive installation. One subject drew a detailed map of the building and grounds layout, the other provided information about the interior including code words, data subsequently verified by sponsor sources [i.e. CIA].'[44]

What Price had described turned out to be a satellite interrogation station, which eavesdropped on Soviet space vehicles; the code words referred to those operations. The CIA scientist monitoring the test, a physiologist from the research and development side of the agency, believed he had a potential class 'A' espionage agent who could roam psychically anywhere in the world, ferreting out secrets undetected.[45]

The CIA's contract study on the Soviet efforts, 'Novel Bio-physical Information Transfer Mechanism' (NBIT) was published on 14 January 1975. It concluded: 'The Russians may now be implementing the next logical step [to experiments proposed five years earlier – author], namely to reinforce, enhance, or aid NBIT in certain trained or gifted individuals after having discovered the basic communications carriers.' The DIA's follow-up reports reinforced this, warning that: 'Soviet or Czech perfection of psychotronic weapons would pose a severe threat to enemy military, embassy or security functions. The emitted energy would be silent and difficult to detect electronically. The Soviets claim to have developed effective biological energy sensors and the only power source required would be the human operator.'[46]

Remote viewing work therefore continued. Pat Price was asked on several occasions to provide his services to the Office of Naval Intelligence [ONI], as well as the National Security Agency.[47]

For several years after Ingo Swann's success in SCANATE, he trained selected individuals with possible psychic abilities from the military and intelligence to become psychic spies.[48] Even high-ranking officers such as Major General Thompson [Assistant Chief of Staff for Intelligence, 1977-91], Jack Vorona [DIA], and Major General Albert Stubblebine, were remote viewing guinea pigs.[49]

The SRI remote viewers were studied by top physicists. Ingo Swann and Uri Geller surprised Nobel laureate Brian Josephson, who first developed the Josephson junction, the basis for measuring biomagnetism. Both of them managed to deflect the SQUID [the needle on a chart recorder] to such a degree that Josephson, like Evan Harris Walker, suggested that physics needed to adopt a new paradigm to incorporate hidden variables and universal intelligence.[50]

In the early 1970s Evan Harris Walker tried to incorporate psi phenomena within the framework of quantum mechanics. Walker's theory links consciousness to the hidden variables of quantum theory. He also referred to the psychic deformation of material objects in his work, specifically to the magnetometer tests at SRI with Ingo Swann. He stated that the magnitude of PK (Psychokinesis : metal bending) effects on SRI magnetometer achieved by Ingo Swann agreed with theoretical calculations. Helmut Schmidt, a physicist responsible for many of the innovative experiments which have made the connection between psi and quantum mechanics, has also proposed a theory of psi function based on quantum mechanical principals.[51]

David Bohm, another prominent physicist who personally studied Geller – like his colleagues Henry Margenau and O. Costa Beauregard – has repeatedly stated there is nothing in quantum physics that forbids psi phenomena. De Beauregard maintains that certain axioms of quantum physics virtually demand that psi phenomena exist.[52] Eugine Wigner, a Nobel prize winner, and Prof. John Taylor (Kings College, London), both argued that Geller's effects may arise from low frequency electromagnetic radiation produced by the heart, brain and muscles, proving the West's increasing convergence with the Soviet psi studies.[53]

The literature indicates that the US military misled both Congress and the media at the time of these experiments because of growing concern for psychic security. Concern was expressed by Ron Robertson, a security officer at Lawrence Livermore Laboratory in California. Robertson, who had followed psychic developments in an official capacity, seriously feared that a talented psychic might trigger or disable a warhead merely by psychokinetic force of mind:

'All it takes is the ability to move one-eighth of an ounce, a quarter of an inch at a distance of one foot,' he warned.[54]

Under 'Congressional pressure on the Defense Department to fund its own psychic research programme, the Pentagon's Advanced Researched Project Agency (ARPA) decided to evaluate Geller at SRI in 1972 to determine if any further testing warranted Pentagon money.'[55] The Pentagon decision was taken after Geller had spent four successful weeks of experiments with some of the world's leading physicists and psychologists at SRI in November and December 1972.

The ARPA team, led by George Lawrence, Deputy Director of Human Resources at ARPA, included Ray Hyman, a frequent consultant to the Department of Defense and the Science Foundation, and Gerry Shore, both of whom were amateur magicians. Their evaluation was negative and Geller was accused of fraud and using magic tricks.

However, their evaluation was deliberately flawed.

For example, instead of blindfolding Geller, as SRI had always done when asked to telepathically identify drawings, he was asked to cover his eyes with his hands. They then accused him of peeking.[56]

SRI later vehemently criticised ARPA's review and called it a debacle.[57] Hyman filed a report with the Department of Defense and sent a copy to Martin Gardner at the Scientific American in which Targ and Puthoff were hoping to publish their findings.[58] Three months after ARPA's review, Leon Jaroff published an article in Time, presenting Targ and Puthoff as sloppy researchers and Geller as a fraud.

Others like James Randi, and more recently retired Colonel John Alexander, who was the chief of Advanced Human Technology Office, US Army Intelligence and Security Command, and Director of Advanced Systems Concepts Office, US Army Laboratory Command, have followed this line. Alexander was fully aware of psi work throughout his career, but in his book, 'The Warrior's Edge', he refers to a series of trivialities. Yet, as a NATO advisor on the more serious aspects of psi-related weapons – some now categorised as non-lethal weapons – he wanted to classify research in this field.[59]

Despite a campaign of disinformation by US military and intelligence, the US House of Representatives' Committee on Science and Technology in June 1981 released a 530-page study, based on two years research. It was entitled 'Survey of Science and Technology Issues Present and Future' and stated: 'In the area of national defense, there are obvious implications of one's ability to identify distant sites and affect sensitive instruments or other humans. A general recognition of the degree of inter-connectiveness of minds could have far-reaching social and political implications for this nation and the world.' Two years later another report, from the Congressional Research Service, entitled 'Research into 'Psi' Phenomena: Current Status and Trends of Congressional Concern', echoed the same views.

In 1982, Major General Albert Stubblebine, Director of US Army Intelligence and Security Command (INSCOM), a keen psi believer, employed several psychics to remote view the house of Panamanian General Manuel Noriega, who was suspected of channelling arms from Nicaraguan Sandanistas to El Salvadorian leftist guerrillas. Remote viewers managed to scan Noreiga's house, and provide a detailed, two page report of the rooms and their contents.

In response to my Freedom of Information Act (FOIA) request for records specifically concerning INSCOM, a letter of 4 October 1994 informed me that: 'The results of searches revealed no records concerning Operation/Project Landbroker.' Eventually, on 25 August 1995, INSCOM released relevant records concerning this project. A SECRET/NOFORN[60] letter, dated 17 March 1988, from the Office of the Deputy Chief of Staff for Intelligence, and signed by Col. Donald F. Ullmann, GS, Chief, HUMINT Division, makes it clear that it was a 'black' project: 'Though official files for Project LANDBROKER do not exist at INSCOM, [and there is no] information on the Project in material sequestered in conjunction with YELLOW FRUIT cases, some material was retained by ADCSOPS-H Desk Office.' The letter adds, 'Part 1 of the Project involved an attempt to conduct a psychic penetration of a residence that was used by Noriega as a meeting site.'

Another SECRET/NOFORN letter from US Army Intelligence and Security Command, signed by Brigadier General Ira C. Owens, Deputy Commander, dated 29 February 1996, describes the project: 'In 1983 this Headquarters initiated a project named LAND-BROKER. The project appears to have been at the direction of M.G. Stubblebine (then CG INSCOM). The effort was conducted by the Quick Reaction Team (QRT) of the ADCSOPS-OPSEC staff. This was an offensive intelligence collection operation broken down into four parts, designed to collect information using psychic penetrations. LANDBROKER projects were always targeted against foreign nationals and never involved US citizens.'[61]

Today, US military and intelligence have projects, identified only by numbers, which monitor the progress, research and development of psychic research worldwide. Information gathered through various Department of Defense sections is directed up to the DIA for final evaluation.

Command (INSCOM) Project 260130: For several years through their information gathering mission of Project 260130, INSCOM have been collecting information on a wide range of topics in relation to paranormal topics and psychic warfare. On 18 August 1995, in response to my inquiry concerning the use of psychics in matters relating to operations, projects, studies, or programmes, INSCOM released documents concerning the: 'activities of the Japan Psychotronics Institute, a parapsychology organization affiliated with the International Association for Psychotronics Research, located in Czechoslovakia.' Previously released records show similar intelligence interest in other countries including China, Russia, Czechoslovakia, Hungary, Romania, former East Germany, Bulgaria and North Korea. Reports are dispatched to the DIA for final evaluation for their intelligence value. Most of them are gathered from human intelligence sources. Copies of these reports, in addition to a host of DoD military components, are also sent to the CIA and NSA.[62]

Command (INSCOM) Project 223310: Not much is known about this project, except it also collects information on paranormal topics in relation to psychic warfare. INSCOM informed me in their letter of 24 April 1995, that this project has been on-going for 25 years.[63] The records released show that one of the main missions of this project is/was to obtain pertinent information from serious sources who are prepared or encouraged to defect. West Germany then seemed to be one crossing point for that purpose.[64]

US Air Force project 140410, is also similarly tasked. Unevaluated reports gathered by the Air Force are sent to Air Intelligence Agency and DIA. The DIA has the final responsibility for their evaluation.[65]

It is now clear that both Russia and the US, whilst publicly down-playing its seriousness, continued their psychic research for decades. They followed progress using their intelligence agencies, and for years whispered ignorance in public forums. The next chapter will move on to delve further into the CIA's interest in remote viewing, and their evaluating its use for intelligence purposes.

Footnotes:

1. Arthur Lyons and Marcello Truzzi Phd., 'Blue Sense; Psychic Detectives and Crime', (Mysterious Press, New York 1991).

2. CIA released records on ESP to author – 1987. On this and related areas see 'On Some Matters of Concern in Psychic Research' by Michael Rossman, in John White, (ed.) 'Psychic Warfare: Fact or Fiction?' (The Acquarian Press, London 1988), especially pp. 84/5 which discusses some of the documents released to me.

3. 'Psychological Phenomena Applicable To The Development of Psychological Weapons', Clifford P. Hahn and staff, American Institute of Research, Washington Office, December 1965; prepared for Directorate of Armament Development. Research and Technology Division, Air Force Systems Command, Eglin Air Force Base, Florida.

4. According to documents released to author in August 1995, from Technical Support Working Group (TSWG), of the US State Department, in January 1994, there were a total of 95 projects – of which 23 are operational, 5 follow-on development pursued in TSWG, 10 follow-on development pursued by another agency; 7 projects were completed, 4 were completed and proved not viable therefore terminated, 42 active projects not yet operational, and 4 new starters.

5. On Vasiliev see 'Distant Influence' by Anita Gregory in White (ed) op. cit. 2.

6. I have a CIA released, untitled memorandum dated 15 March 1963 headed 'Proposed Visit of Source to USSR'. Point three of the memo states: 'We would be particularly interested in all data and publications he may be able to accumulate with particular reference to the field of ESP.' Although the name of the source has been removed I believe it to be Pratt.

7. S. Ostrander and L. Schroeder, 'Psychic Discoveries Behind the Iron Curtain', (Prentice-Hall, New Jersey, 1970).

8. Anita Gregory, Introduction to Leonid Vasiliev's 'Experiments in Distant Influence', (E. P. Dutton, New York, 1974), p. 54.

9. Michael Rossman, op. cit. 2, p. 117.

10. A recently released, untitled document from the US Office of Naval Intelligence shows that the US knew that despite the official Soviet line, which resulted in the closure of a number of notable psychic research laboratories, the Soviets continued their research. Records released by the Office of Naval Intelligence to the author in August 1995.

11. For example, the research at the Maimonides Hospital in New York. This is discussed in 'A Close-up Look at Remote Viewing', Ingo Swann, 6 December 1995 – Internet. In the aftermath of the CIA's public announcement, Swann has published several articles on the InterNet. Swann's accounts are carefully chosen to follow the official line. For more information on Swann, also see his 'Your Nostradamus Factor' (Simon and Schuster, New York, 1993).

12. 'A Close-up Look at Remote Viewing', Ingo Swann, 6 December 1995 – Internet.

13. A May 1992, Defense Intelligence Agency (DIA) document, classified Secret/NOFORN, still reflects the US Intelligence community fears about psychic research: 'Photography and available open source literature concerning the scope and thrust of the Chinese PS [parapsychology – author] effort. Collection Efforts are an attempt to update DIA holdings and plug a 5-10 year intelligence gap in this area.'

14. Among the half dozen senators supporting the programme, were Clairborne Pell [Democrat-Rhode Island] and Robert C. Byrd [Democrat-West Virginia]. In the course of the programme, C. Richard D'Amoto, Senator Byrd's staff member, and an intelligence specialist, several times successfully quashed DIA's effort to kill the RV programme.

15. British newspapers gave a variety of figures. The Sunday Times, 3 December 1995, quoted the figure $12 million, and Guardian, 30 September 1995, quoted a figure of $11 million.

16. 'Novel Biophysical Information Transfer Mechanism (NBIT)', Final Report, 14 January 1975. Records released to author by the CIA.

17. Ronald M. McRae, 'Mind Wars', (St. Martin Press, New York, 1984), p. 3.

18. Stanley Krippner, 'Human Possibilities; Mind Exploration in the USSR and Eastern Europe', (Doubleday, New York,1981), pp. 161-2.

19. McRae, op. cit. 17, p. 56. McDonnell Aerospace Foundation was founded by James McDonnell of McDonnell Douglas Corp. McRae does not mention the name of the CIA conduit in his work.

20. Ibid. p. 2. The US Navy had employed 34 psychics on this work.

21. J. Gaither Pratt, 'ESP Research Today', (Scarecrow Press, NY, 1973), pp. 55-83.

22. Richard Broughton, 'Parapsychology; The Controversial Science', (Ballantine Books, New York, 1991), pp. 102, 105 and 6.

23. Contract 953653 under NAS7-100, SRI Project 2613. Report titled 'Development of Techniques to Enhance Man/Machine Communication.' NASA contract to SRI began in 1973, through the Jet Propulsion Laboratory, an unincorporated division of the California Institute of Technology – CALTECH.

24. Broughton op. cit. 22, pp. 40 and 322.

25. Ostrander and Shroeder, op. cit. 7, p. 29.

26. 'The Emergence of Project SCANATE; The First Espionage-

worthy Remote Viewing Experiment – Summer 1973'. Ingo Swann, 29 December 1995, InterNet.

27. See Mind to Mind, Rene Warcollier, (Creative Age Press, NY 1946).

28. See 'Exploring the Ultra-Perceptive Faculty', J. Hittinger, (Rider & Co., London, 1941).

29. Ingo Swann interview on 'Dreamland' transcribed Organization: University of Wisconsin, 12 December 1996. Russell Targ also confirmed that some RV work was done on the Soviet's submarine, but the result was never fed back to them due to the classified nature of the relevant programme. (Telephone conversation with Targ, 23 April 1996.)

30. A similar experiment was conducted in Paul McKenna's 'Paranormal' TV show 19 February 1996. Joseph McMoneagle, a former Army Intelligence officer, was the Remote Viewer.

31. Ingo Swann interview on 'Dreamland' transcribed Organization (sic; transcription from Swann) University of Wisconsin, 12 December 1996.

32. Janet Mitchell, (McFarland, New York, 1981).

33. Swann, op. cit. 22.

34. 'Remote Viewing as One of Sidhis', Ingo Swann, 10 January 1996, InterNet. Also see 'The Expanding World of Human Perception', Robert Rivlin and Karen Gravelle, (Simon and Schuster, New York, 1984).

35. DIA called this method Target Phenomenology.

36. Chipman had been Chief of Operations of Nha Trang Office called the Combined Studies Detachment, in Vietnam, had previously been stationed in Moscow, Berlin and Miami, and had served in Sumatra [Indonesia], Korea, Philippines and Laos. Chipman is the subject of four citations as a CIA officer in Daniel Brandt's NameBase. Information on Foote from private sources.

37. A. Puharich, 'Beyond Telepathy', (Doubleday, Garden City, New York, 1962).

38. A. Puharich, 'The Sacred Mushroom', (Doubleday, Garden City, New York, 1959).

39. Truzzi and Lyons, op. cit. 1, p. 114.

40. Uri Geller and Guy Lyon Playfair, 'The Geller Effect', (Grafton, London, 1988), p. 244.

41. 'In 1984, columnist Jack Anderson published a series of articles on a CIA project codenamed Grill Flame ' [which] had produced information later verified by satellite about a very sensitive nuclear test site at Semipalatinsk in Soviet Kazakhstan, and had led to the location of a crashed Soviet TU-95 'Backfire' bomber somewhere in Africa.' Geller and Lyon Playfair, op. cit. 40, p. 342. The accuracy of this information was later verified by spy satellites.

42. Russell Targ and Harold E. Puthoff, 'Mind Reach: Scientists Look at Psychic Ability', (Delacorte, New York, 1977) p. 52.

43. John L. Wilhelm,'Psychic Spying' in 'Washington Post' (Sunday Magazine) 7 August 1977.

44. 'The First CIA-Selected Coordinate Remote Viewing', Ingo Swann, undated – InterNet; and 'Category I: Long Distance Remote Viewing', p.4, classified Secret.

45. Ibid.

46. 'Biological Effects of Electromagnetic Radiation (Radio Waves and Microwaves) – Eurasian communist Countries', Defense Intelligence Agency, October 1976. One such recent device is called Elipton, of which Profesor Vlail Kaznacheyev said: 'Sensors of the Elipton act on eyes and ears and transform scenery and sounds into bio-flows which are transmitted into space towards cosmic regulators. By targeting these signals to sensitive receivers and decoders, they could be used to collect information for military, scientific or political intelligence. Once the target [a human being] is included in the intelligence gathering system, or any other phase of the weapon, he becomes its slave. This could lead him to the state where he would execute any order, including suicide – such is the power of the Elipton.'

47. Confidential sources.

48. The individuals concerned and their periods of service in this field are: Sgt. Lyn Buchanan, 1983-92, Sgt. Mel Riley, 1978-90, Ingo Swann, 1972-89, Major Edward Dames, 1984-89.

49. Telephone conversation with Major Edward Dames, and ONI sources. Jack Verona referred to the RV experiments in a letter to the Independent on 1 Sunday October 1995.

50. McRae, op. cit. 17, pp. 78-79, and Brian Josephson speaking on the BBC World Service radio programme 'The Unexplained', 5 May 1987.

51. See Evan H. Walker, 'Measurement in Quantum Mechanics Revisited'; Response to Phillip's 'Criticism of the Quantum Mechanical Theory of Psi', Journal of the American Society for Psychical Research, 1987, No. 81, pp. 333-369; and Helmut Schmidt,'The Strange Properties of Psychokinesis', Journal of Scientific Exploration, 1987, No. 1, pp. 103-118, and 'Collapse of the State Vector and PK Effects' in Foundation of Physics, no. 12 (1982) pp. 565-581.

52. O. Casta de Beauregard, 'Quantum Paradoxes and Aristotle's Twofold Information Concept', in Laura Oteri (ed.), Quantum Physics and Para-psychology, (New York Parapsychology Foundation, 1975), pp. 91-102. See also Broughton op. cit. 22, p. 75.

53. M. Carlyn, 'An Assessment of the Myers-Briggs Type Indicator', Journal of Personality Assessment, 1977, No. 41, pp. 461-473. Taylor placed a small crystal of lithium fluoride in a plastic container. Geller held his hands several inches over the container. Within ten seconds the crystal shattered into several pieces. Taylor stated that there was no chance for Geller to have touched the crystal, since at all times during the experiment he could see a gap between Geller's hand and the container. Since then, apparently, under severe peer pressure, Taylor has recanted and apparently now believes that although he saw what he saw, and is unable to explain how the fraud was carried out, it must have been a fraud.

54. Wilhelm op. cit. 43.

55. McRae op. cit. 17, pp. 49 and 80-81.

56. Ibid. p. 84

57. Ibid. p. 82.

58. Geller and Lyon Playfair, op. cit. 40, p. 261.

59. Col. John B. Alexander, Major Richard Groller and Janet Morris, 'The Warrior's Edge', (William Morrow and Company Inc., New York, 1990). Janet Morris split with Alexander because he wanted to classify it. See 'Wired' February 1995 for the split. See also Steven Aftergood, 'The Soft-Kill Fallacy' in The Bulletin of Atomic Scientists, September/October 1994.

60. NOFORN: no foreigners.

61. Records released by the US Army Security and Intelligence Command, August 1995.

62. Records released to author by the US Army Intelligence and Security Command, 1995.

63. I was initially asked to pay the sum of $2,075,000 (!) for the costs of copying the documents.

64. Records released to the author by the US Army Intelligence and Security Command, 1995.

65. Correspondence with US Air Force Air Intelligence Agency, USAF/AIA, 24 January, 14 April, and 17 August 1995.

The Mind Controllers

Chapter Ten

Operation Star Gate

In July 1995 the CIA went public, and declared its interest in so-called Remote Viewing (RV),[1] the ability to spy on remote sites telepathically. As a result, much new information suddenly became available. At the time of the announcement of its role in this area, the CIA and US Department of Defense had a twenty-two year operational track record in RV; the CIA was involved from 1973 to 1977 (with initial studies beginning in 1972), and the DoD/DIA from 1977 to 1995. Initially, the operational aspects of RV, in other words using it for intelligence gathering, were fairly enmeshed with research into the field, although in later years, the two areas became more distinct.

In 1995 the CIA declassified and released documents to Russell Targ which concerned their sponsorship of their 1970s programme at Stanford Research Institute in Melano Park, California.[2] On 6 September 1995, the Public Affairs Bureau of the Agency released the following statement regarding that agency's role in Remote Viewing:

'As mandated by Congress, CIA is reviewing available information and past research programs concerning parapsychological phenomena, mainly 'Remote Viewing' to determine whether they might have any utility for intelligence collection.

'CIA sponsored research on this subject in the 1970s.

'– At that time, the program, always considered speculative and controversial, was determined to be unpromising.

– CIA is also in the process of declassifying the program's history.

'We expect to complete the current review this autumn and to make a recommendation regarding any future work by the US Intelligence community in this area.' Pursuant to the statement, and at the request of the Senate Appropriations Committee, in June 1995, the CIA's Office of Research and Development [ORD], commissioned the American Institute of Research (AIR) to conduct a review of the CIA's Star Gate programme (the official mandate was to 'explore and exploit a parapsychological phenomenon known as 'remote viewing' in support of the US Intelligence community.'[3]) Star Gate's initial mission was three-fold:

1. To assess similar foreign programmes in the field of remote viewing.

2. Through contractors to conduct research into the existence, as well as cause and effect of this phenomenon.

3. To seek and see if RV could be used as an intelligence tool.

All RV programmes were suspended in spring 1995 due to a shift in policy regarding the field of research. However, when exercises were conducted earlier, results of multiple viewings would be summarised in three or four page reports, which were then sent to the agency that originally commissioned the viewing. But, from 1994 onwards, recipient agencies of RV reports were formally asked to evaluate the accuracy and value of the contents. And seemingly, results did not meet the standard updated, intelligence requirements.

Regarding the AIR review: 'To evaluate the research program, a 'blue-ribbon' panel was assembled. The panel included two noted experts in the area of parapsychology: Dr Jessica Utts, a Professor of Statistics at the University of California at Davis, and Dr Raymond Hyman,[4] a Professor of Psychology at the University of Oregon. In addition to their extensive credentials, they were selected to represent both sides of the paranormal controversy: Dr Utts has published articles that view paranormal interpretation positively, while Dr Hyman was selected to represent a more sceptical position.'[5]

AIR also included two of its senior scientists on the panel; Dr Lincoln Moses, an Emeritus Professor at Stanford University, to provide statistical advice, and Dr David A. Goslin, President of AIR, as co-ordinator of the research efforts. 'Panel members were asked to review all laboratory experiments and meta-analytic reviews conducted as part of the research program; this consisted of approximately 80 separate publications, many of which are summary reports of multiple experiments. In the course of this review, special attention was given to those studies that (a) provided the strongest evidence for the remote viewing phenomena, and (b) represented new experiments controlling for methodological artefacts identified in earlier reviews. Separate written reviews were prepared by Dr Utts and Dr Hyman. They exchanged reviews with other panel members who then tried to reach a consensus.'[6]

The AIR Executive Summary made the following conclusions on the research studies into RV conducted in various laboratories:

1. A statistically significant laboratory effort has been demonstrated in the sense that hits occur more often than chance.

2. It is unclear whether the observed effects can unambiguously be attributed to the paranormal ability of the remote viewers, as opposed to characteristics of the judges or of the target or some other characteristic of the methods used. Use of the same remote viewers, the same judge, and the same target photographs makes it impossible to identify their independent effects.

3. Evidence has not been provided that clearly demonstrates that the causes of hits are due to the operation of paranormal phenomena; the laboratory experiments have not identified the origins or nature of the remote viewing phenomenon, if, indeed, it exists at all.

To assess the operational value of remote viewing

in intelligence gathering, AIR applied a three-fold strategy:

First, the relevant research literature was reviewed to identify whether the conditions applying during intelligence gathering would reasonably permit RV.

Second, members of three groups who were involved in the programme were interviewed: (1) end users of the information; (2) the remote viewers providing the reports, and (3) the programme manager.

Third, feedback information obtained from the judgements of end users on the accuracy and value of RV reports was assessed.[7]

The results of these findings are summarised:

1. The conditions under which the remote viewing phenomenon is observed in laboratory settings do not apply in intelligence gathering situations. For example, viewers cannot be provided with feedback and targets may not display the characteristics needed to produce hits.

2. The end users indicated that, although some accuracy was observed with regard to broad background characteristics, the remote viewing reports failed to produce the concrete, specific information valued in intelligence gathering.

3. The information provided was inconsistent, inaccurate with regard to specifics, and required substantial subjective interpretation.

4. In no case had the information provided ever been used to guide intelligence operations. Thus, remote viewing failed to produce actionable intelligence.[8]

The AIR report concluded that although statistically significant effects had been observed in the laboratory, nevertheless, it remained unclear if RV exists as a paranormal phenomenon. It further argued that laboratory experiments have failed to provide scientifically sound evidence as to the nature and the origins of the remote view. AIR therefore rejected continued trials: 'Thus, we conclude that continued use of remote viewing in intelligence gathering is not warranted.'[9]

It should be noted that AIR did not have access to all sensitive, operational documents, which, I am confidently informed, are numerous. Neither could the time frame within which AIR compiled its report be considered sufficient. As Dr Marcello Truzzi commented:

'The recent strange CIA/AIR report on the one hand indicates about a 15% above-chance guessing rate while somehow managing to conclude that RV is not operationally useful (bad enough but also dismissing the many hits in the operational, non-experimental efforts with RV). Given the low reliability of so many espionage methods and sources, one would have expected them to be delighted with 15% over chance. Obviously, the conclusions were dictated in advance of the evaluation study and were mostly politically motivated.'[10]

Dr Edwin C. May, Director of Research for Remote Viewing Programs for both the CIA and the DIA, also believes that the AIR Report was politically motivated, and neither the AIR nor the CIA were given enough time to prepare the document. Dr May also believes that the cancellation of the RV programmes was mainly due to 'the geopolitical shifts', and a corresponding review of priorities by the intelligence community. He speculates on the possibility of maintaining a classified nucleus of remote viewers, and states that while there were half a dozen remote viewers involved in the programme, due to its classified nature of the information he could not name them. He further commented that Dr Jack Vorona, Director of the DIA's RV programme, was one of the Directors who had intimate knowledge of the details of the programme and strongly supported it.[11]

Ingo Swann, who retired from the programme in 1989, believes it took on several more people and became quite busy to run and that some of the people involved did not have the high standards required. According to Swann, Ed Dames was one student, imposed on him for political reasons, who he would rather not have had.[12]

At least as early as 1971, the CIA had been monitoring the results of the ASPR experiments detailed in the last chapter, and had also been comparing them with similar information obtained from the Soviet Union. As a result, the CIA had become convinced that this research was significant.

According to Swann: 'In late October 1971, I and a colleague were in Washington. This was still a time when no one wanted a psychic anywhere near their official premises. So, we met in bars and pizza parlours. On this occasion there were six spooks. But, one seemed very important because when he opened his mouth to talk, everyone else shut up immediately. Actually, he did not say much, but when he did it was always with a pointed question. "Mr. Swann," he said, "If you were going to set up a threat analysis programme to match what the Soviets are up to, what would you do?"[13]

In 1972 Harold Puthoff was involved in laser research at Stanford Research Institute (SRI), now SRI International, in Melano Park, California. At that time he was also circulating a proposal seeking to obtain a grant for some research work in quantum biology. In it he raised the issue of whether physical theory, as it was publicly known, was capable of describing life processes, and had suggested some measurements involving plants and lower organisms.[14]

Cleve Backster received a copy from Puthoff. He was involved in measuring the electrical activity of plants with standard polygraph equipment in New York. Ingo Swann, Backster's friend, saw the proposal during a visit to his laboratory. Subsequently, on 30 March 1972, he wrote to Puthoff suggesting that if he was interested in investigating this subject, he should conduct some experiments in parapsychology. He included in his letter accounts of some of his successes in psychokinesis in Dr Gertrude Schmidler's laboratory at the City College, New York. Puthoff invited Swann to visit SRI for a week in June 1972 and demonstrate these effects.[15]

Prior to Swann's visit, Puthoff concealed a well-shielded magnetometer below the floor of the building. It was used for quark-detection experiments. Its existence seemed to perturb Swann. To Puthoff's surprise, Swann remotely viewed this complex piece of machinery and drew a reasonable outline of its interior working mechanism. Puthoff, impressed by Swann's finding, wrote a paper about this event and circulated it amongst his scientific colleagues.[16]

A few weeks after the publication of his paper, two CIA officers turned up at SRI. They had done their homework on Puthoff's background, and knew about his work as an Officer of Naval Intelligence, and then as a civilian with the National Security Agency (NSA) a few years before. Puthoff was told that there was increasing concern in the CIA about Soviet parapsychology efforts and its KGB, GRU funding. Since parapsychology was considered dubious at best by the Western scientific community, the CIA was looking for a research establishment somewhat outside the academic mainstream to handle a quietly funded and classified, investigative programme. They asked Puthoff if he was willing to conduct some more experiments with Ingo Swann[17] and they indicated that if the results of these tests were encouraging, he would be asked to consider a pilot programme to further this investigation.

Puthoff agreed, and arranged for a series of tests.[18] He commented subsequently: 'Since the reputation of the intelligence services is mixed among members of the general populace, I have on occasion been challenged as to why I would agree to co-operate with the CIA or other elements of the intelligence community in this work. My answer is simply that as a result of my own previous exposure to this community I became persuaded that war can almost always be traced to a failure in intelligence, and that therefore the strongest weapon for peace is good intelligence.'[19]

The first tests at SRI were simple and successful. The CIA officers visiting the lab would ask Swann to describe items they had hidden in a box. As a result of these initial tests, in October 1972, an eight month pilot study programme, with a budget of $49,909, was negotiated. The pilot was known as the Biofields Measurement Program, and it ran from January to August 1973.[20]

One of Puthoff's colleagues, Russell Targ, who had a long history of involvement in parapsychology, joined the team. In the course of this pilot study at SRI, three of the CIA's contract monitors participated as remote viewers in order to assess the protocols. They were contributors to seven of fifty-five viewings during this time, several of striking quality.[21]

By 1975, Puthoff and Targ could report that: 'The development of this capability at SRI has evolved to the point where visiting CIA personnel with no previous exposure to such concepts have performed well under controlled laboratory conditions (that is, generated target descriptions of sufficiently high quality to permit blind matching of descriptions to targets by independent judges).'[22]

One of the most intriguing of the fifty-five SRI experiments was number 46, the second major co-ordinate viewing in the CIA-funded eight month pilot study. The purpose of this experiment was: 'To try to ascertain if long distance remote sensing could extend to a very far distant (sic), to record the time it took before impressions began to be given, and to compare the impressions with published scientific feedback.'[23]

The target chosen was the planet Jupiter; the date of experiment, 27 April 1973. NASA's Pioneer Ten was already en route to the planet, but too far away to send data back to Earth control, principally at Jet

Propulsion Laboratories (JPL). The viewers were Ingo Swann in California, and Harold Sherman in Arkansas.[24]

With two viewers 2000 miles apart, the idea was to see whether the independent data obtained would correspond with each other – which it did. In the course of this attempt, a ring around Jupiter was discovered. 'Very high in the atmosphere there are crystals, they glitter. Maybe the stripes are like bands of crystals, maybe like rings of Saturn, though not far out like that. Very close within the atmosphere. I bet you they'll reflect radio probes. Is that possible if you had a cloud of crystals that were assaulted by different radio waves?'[25] The existence of the ring was discovered and confirmed in early 1979, six years after this experiment. A copy of the 300 page long report of this viewing was sent to a number of scientific institutions including NASA.

On Christmas Day of 1962, the Soviet Union conducted the last of 65 nuclear weapons tests. These tests started on 1 August 1962, and were conducted on and over the mountains of Semipalatinsk and the ice of Novaya Zemlya. Early in 1963, the Soviets signed a Test Ban Treaty, and their testing programme went underground. The big question for the US was: what of the future? The US intelligence community lacked sufficient information concerning the Soviet's nuclear material production, patterns of use, future application and trends.[26]

Pat Price was asked in July 1974 to remote view the Semipalatinsk test region. This was the first official remote viewing project targeting the Soviet Union:

'To determine the utility of remote viewing under operational conditions, a long-distance remote viewing experiment was carried out on a sponsor-designated target of current interest, an unidentified research center at Semipalatinsk, USSR. This experiment was carried out in three phases, was under direct control of the COTR [Contracting Officer's Technical Representative].

'In Phase one, map co-ordinates were furnished to the experimenters, the only additional information provided being the designation of the target as an R&D [Research and Development] test facility. The experimenters then carried out a remote viewing experiment with subject 1 [Pat Price] on a double-blind basis. The results of the experiment were turned over to client representatives for data evaluation.

'Were the results not promising, the experiment would have stopped at this point. The results were judged to be of sufficiently good quality, however, that phase two was entered in which the subject was focused on the generation of physical data which could be client-verified, providing a calibration in the process. The end of phase two gradually evolved into the first part of the phase three, the generation of unverifiable data not available to the client, but of interest nonetheless. Evaluation of the data by the client is under way.'[27]

Some of the results of RV experiments were startling. On a Night Line TV show on 28 November 1995, a CIA representative, known only as 'Norm',*[28] a former CIA Technical Advisor to John McMahon, Deputy Director, on the use of RV programmes in mid-1980s, stated, 'Well, if it is the eight martini results you want to talk about, I won't talk about them.' "Eight martini results" was an in-house term for remote viewing data so good it cracked everyone's sense of reality. On the same programme Robert Gates, ex-Director of the CIA, added that RV had a promising future.

Ingo Swann has provided an account of one such eight martini result, which took place between 1975/76.[29] He was asked to remote view Soviet submarines.[30] According to Swann, 'there was all sorts of brass sitting there and Puthoff was on my left and this two or three star general was on my right and I was fussing away as they gave me the co-ordinates. This was one of those 'big tests' things that went on, with witnesses and the room was filled. And so I was doing my remote viewing bugaloo and finally I came across something that I stopped in my tracks and I looked at it and said, 'Oh my God'. So I whispered over Hal's ear and said 'Hal, I don't know what to do. I think that this submarine has shot down a UFO or the UFO fired on her. What shall I do?'

'And Puthoff was as pale as anything you know, and he looked at me and whispered, "Oh, Christ. It's your show. You do what you think you should do." So, I sketched out this picture of this UFO and this brass sitting on my right grabbed it and said, "What's that, Mr. Swann?" I said, "Sir, I think it is rather obvious what that is." And he took that paper and he stood up, and when he stood up everybody else stood up, except me and Puthoff, and walked out of the room, so did the others. So Puthoff and I went back to the hotel and I said, "Oh Christ, we've blown the programme." So we went out and got drunk on margaritas and things like that and went back. Three days later Puthoff got a call. The call said, "OK, how much money do you want"?'[31]

The 'Anomalous Mental Phenomena' programmes which were carried out at SRI from 1973 through 1989, were continued in SAIC from 1992 through 1994. A memorandum issued on 25 July 1995 by Dr Edwin C. May provided titles and details of the ten experiments which were carried out at SAIC.[32] The title of these experiments are: Target Dependencies; AC with Binary Coding; AC Lucid Dreams, base; AC Lucid Dreams, pilot; ERD AC Behaviour, Entropy II.[33] Other experiments carried out in SAIC were: AC of Binary Targets; MEG Replication; Remote Observation; ERD EEG Investigation.[34]

As mentioned, one of the operational sections of the RV programme was the DoD project GRILL FLAME. Records were denied to me by several US Intelligence community member organisations. Eventually, on 1 February 1996, I managed to obtain relevant documents regarding this little-known project. These records were located and declassified pursuant to a request on 7 December 1995 by US Intelligence and Security Command.

The operational aspects of STAR GATE – the overall programme – can be traced back to 1977, when the US Army set out to use RV to discover what intelligence information could be discovered about the enemy. The Assistant Deputy Chief of Staff – Operations; Human Intelligence branch (ADCSOPS-HUMINT) through its Special Action Branch, was given this mission. By 1978, Detachment 'G' was established, which was later listed in the Intelligence and Security Command [INSCOM] books as GRILL FLAME. The US Army was now given a new mission: to utilise RV as an intelligence gathering tool. By this time, the entire DoD's RV programme was moved under the administrative umbrella of GRILL FLAME; a joint effort by several US departments and agencies, with the DIA's oversight.[35]

In 1983, Detachment G [GRILL FLAME], whose personnel and operations had been trained by Ingo Swann, parted company with him. Major Ed Dames had managed to put together a team apparently capable of producing the required data. This separation created a bitter dispute between the two men, which continues today.

The new team under the designation CENTER LANE continued its operations. In 1986, after several controversies, the newly appointed INSCOM commanding general, on the orders of his superiors, moved this unit to the Defense Intelligence Agency. They merged with SUN STREAK, which was under the control of DIA's Scientific and Technical Intelligence Directorate (DT-S).[36]

In the early nineties the RV programme had been reclassified from SAP (Special Access Program) to LIMIDS (Limited Distribution), and was once more re-designated, this time also as STAR GATE. Of 40 personnel officially serving throughout the duration of the programme, 23 were military. In the eighties, when it was at its peak, it employed seven full-time viewers, supported by teams of administrative and analytical personnel.

During the history of RV, there have been a number of sensitive operations. To name a few: BLUE BIRD, that targeted Libyan leader Moammar Gadaffi;[37] LANDBRO-KER, targeting Panamanian General Manuel Noriega;[38] Project THORN, dealing with the UFO problem; and Project ARROW SHOP, about which little is known.

The second phase of Project STAR GATE, which was mainly under DIA's control, used three individuals, two of whom were women. The demise of the programme could be mainly attributed to WRV, Written Remote Viewing, which was introduced in 1988. To the dismay of the original viewers in the other programme, it rapidly became flavour of the month.

WRV was a combination of what was called chan-nelling and automatic writing, as well the use of tarot cards. WRV produced much less reliable results than that of the SRI-developed CRV (Coordinated Remote Viewing) and ERV (Extended Remote Viewing), described as a hybrid relaxation/meditative-based method.

WRV was immediately adopted by the intelligence community as their main modus operandi in this area though, compared to CRV and ERV, it lacked the neces-sary laboratory-based trials. At the time of its transfer from DIA to CIA in June 1995, the STAR GATE programme was left with only three viewers, two using WRV, and only one using CRV. Mismanagement also plagued the programme during its latter years.

During the programme's lifetime from 1986 (its first phase) to the spring of 1995 (second phase), it received more than 200 tasks from operational military organisations, asking them to use RV to attain informa-tion unavailable from other sources. STAR GATE's support waned over time, even though it had clocked up considerable successes. As one intelligence source commented: 'In the historical files there are also a number of customer evaluations from the likes of the

Secret Service, NSA, the Military Services, Joint Chiefs of Staff, and ironically the CIA, reporting (occasionally even in rather glowing terms) the usefulness of remote viewing as an intelligence tool.'[39]

During the past 22 years, RV programmes, backed by continuous research and the help of several hundred scientists from various disciplines, generated a wealth of valuable research data. It should not be discarded for current political reasons. Putting aside their overt military and intelligence applications, the vast array of information generated is a testimony to the fact that humans are not limited to their five sense 'prison'.

Footnotes:

1. While in letters of 22 July and 27 November 1992, the CIA had previously denied to the author having any documents on this subject, it has now admitted to possessing over one hundred thousand pages of records.

2. Copies of these documents were sent to me in August 1995.

On 27 August 1995, by a curious coincidence, Channel 4 in Britain screened the documentary 'The Real X-Files' on the RV programme in the UK (later shown in US), nicely preparing the ground further for their public announcement. 'The Real X-Files' was written by Jim Schnabel who had previously been involved in the debunking of the crop circle phenomenon, and, in his book Dark White, of the alien abduction allegations. Schnabel was introduced to Ingo Swann by two of Swann's friends. (Telephone conversation with Swann, 31 March and 6 April 1996.)

Amongst others participating in CIA/DoD RV programmes were Dr Christopher 'Kit' Green, and Jeoff Harrison, both from Directorate of Intelligence (Office of Science and Technology), CIA – now retired. For Kit Green see Chapter 13.

3. Reuter, Washington, DC, 28 November 1995.

4. For Hyman see Chapter 8.

5. 'An Evaluation of Remote Viewing: Research and Applications', by Michael D. Mumford, Phd., Andrew M. Rose, Phd., David A. Goslin, Phd.; prepared by The American Institute of Research (AIR), 29 September 1995. Executive Summary; Research Evaluation, p. E-2. After the publication of this report in January 1996, Congress, with the DoD and CIA, halted further funding for psyhic research.

6. On 19 April 1996 I wrote to David Goslin, AIR President asking him 17 questions concerning the manner in which AIR had handled their RV report. In his reply of 26 April Goslin wrote, 'I find your questions to be insulting', and asserted that through-out AIR's history it had maintained the highest standards of integrity and scientific objectivity.

7. Op. cit. 5, Executive Summary [Operational Evaluation], AIR report, p. E-3.

8. Ibid., p. E-4.

9. Ibid – [Conclusions], p. E-4.

10. Dr Marcello Truzzi letter of 17 March 1996, to author.

11. Telephone Conversation with Dr Edwin C. May, 6 April 1996. Dr May added that there is a great deal of on-going research regarding the EEG of the remote viewers that as yet has not been published. After Jack Vorona, Director of Department of Defense RV programs STARGATE and CENTER LANE until 1986, Dale Graff, a civilian Physicist from Office of Scientific and Technical Intelligence Directorate DT-S, DIA, took over the directorship of the SUN STREAK RV programme.

12. Ingo Swann commented that most of Ed Dames' RV work at that time, and since the establishment of PSI-TECH lacked any positive feedback. (Telephone conversation with Swann, 4 May 1996). Swann is also critical of Dames' RV work on UFOs. Yet Swann himself has been involved in remote viewing UFOs. In particular he has conducted extensive RV work on the Roswell incident. He prepared his first official remote viewing report on Roswell on 28 April 1993, when four remote viewers were involved. As recently as April this year he was still involved in remote viewing the UFO phenomenon and the alleged aliens. (Copies of his UFO RV work are in my archives.) Russell Targ

also believes that none of the RV work done by the Ed Dames group had any positive outcome. Telephone conversation with Russell Targ, 23 April 1996.

13. 'Messages Regarding Remote Viewing; For the Glory of our Species', Ingo Swann, InterNet, 10 December 1995.

14. 'Toward a Quantum Theory of Life Process', unpublished paper by H.E. Puthoff, 1972 – SRI.

15. Swann visited SRI twice in 1972; in June, and October.

16. A version of this paper, 'Physics, Entropy and Psychokinesis', by Puthoff, H.E. and Targ, R., was later published in Proceedings of the Conference in Quantum Physics and Parapsychology, 1975 (Geneva, Switzerland), New York, Parapsychology Foundation.

17. 'CIA-Initiated Remote Viewing Programme at Stanford Research Institute', H.E. Puthoff, in Journal for Society for Scientific Exploration, Vol. 10. No. 1, 1996, (from draft copy – p.3.). Another interesting point is the connection of the Church of Scientology, a CIA conduit, at least in the early days. When Puthoff was a graduate student at Berkeley he testified on behalf of L. Ron Hubbard's E-Meter. Puthoff, Swann and Edwin May were allegedly members of the Church of Scientology.

18. 'CIA-Initiated Remote Viewing Programme at Stanford Research Institute', H.E. Puthoff, in 'Journal for Society for Scientific Exploration', Vol. 10. No. 1, 1996.

19. Op. cit. 5.

20. 'A Perceptual Channel for Information Transfer over Kilometer Distances: Historical Perspective and Recent Research', H.E. Puthoff, R. Targ, in Proceedings of the Institute of Electrical and Electronic Engineers, 1976.

21. Op. cit. 5.

22. 'Perceptual Augmentation Techniques [Classified; Secret], Part One – Executive Summary. Final Report Covering the Period Jan. 74 through Feb. 75', H.E. Puthoff, and Russell Targ. Electronics and Bioengineering Laboratory, SRI Project 3183. Approved by Earle Jones, Director, Electronics and Bioengineering Lab., Bonner Cox, Executive Director, Information

Science and Engineering Division. Records released by the CIA, 1995.

Also, in the mid-1970s, the CIA requested a lengthy examination of the RV, in which some viewers as well as a number of professional consultants were involved. The result was a report titled 'Social Resistance to Psi'. 'Remote Viewing vs. Its Skeptics', Ingo Swann, 20 January 1996, Internet.

In 1988 an analysis was made of all the experiments at SRI from 1973 until that time – 1988. The analysis was based on all 154 experiments conducted during that era, consisting of over 26,000 individual trials. Of those, almost 20,000 were of the forced choice type and just over a 1000 were laboratory remote viewing. There were a total of 227 subjects in all experiments. 'An Overall Analysis of the SRI Experiments: 1973-88', pp. 3-14. See also SRI International Technical Report, March 1989, 'Review of the Psychoenergetic Research Conducted at SRI International (1973-88)' by May et al. Other remote viewers of this era are Keith Harary, a Tiburon psychologist who joined SRI in 1980, and later continued his work with SAIC (SAIC is discussed below); Larissa Vilenskaya, a Russian emigrant who worked as a psychic in the Soviet Union from 1969 to 1975 and later joined SRI; and Joseph McMoneagle who obtained a Legion of Merit award in 1984 for providing 150 essential elements of information through RV, of value to US defense.

23. 'The 1973 Remote Viewing Probe of The Planet Jupiter', Ingo Swann. 12 December 1995, InterNet.

24. Harold Sherman was a psychic who, in the late 1930s, had taken part in long distance viewing experiments between New York City and the Arctic. These experiments were conducted in conjunction with the Arctic explorer Sir Hubert Wilkins. See 'Thoughts Through Space, Sir Hubert Wilkins and Harold M. Sherman', (Creative Age Press, New York, 1942).

25. Op. Cit. 23. Ms. Beverly Humphrey, a Research Associate and Statistical Analyst, SRI Radio Physics Lab., prepared a Formal Report on behalf of Puthoff and Targ. The report was 300 pages long, and was widely distributed. Also, see Mind Reach, H.E. Puthoff and Russell Targ, Russell, Delacorate Press/Eleanor Friede, New York, 1977.

26. 'DC Power and Cooling Tower', Henry Rubenstein, in Studies in Intelligence, CIA, vol. 16, No. 3, (Autumn 1972), pp. 81,82. Classified Secret. Also, see Inside CIA's Private World, By; H. Bradford Westerfield, Yale University Press, 1995, p. 3.

27. Progress Report No. 5, Covering Period 1 April to August 1974 – Project Atlas Remote Viewing, p. 2. Also, see, Final Report January 1974 through February 1975, Programme Results; Applied Research Efforts, pp. 8 and 9.

28. Norman Jackson.

29. In his telephone conversation of 10 April 1996, with the author, Swann claimed that all of his RVs were of 8-martini grade.

30. Russell Targ confirmed that some RV work was done on the Soviets' submarines, but the result was never fed back to them due to the classified nature of the relevant programme. Telephone conversation with Targ, 23 April 1996.

31. Ingo Swann interview on 'Dreamland' transcribed Organization (sic; literal transcription): University of Wisconsin, 12 December 1996.

32. One of main partners of Science Application International Corporation (SAIC) is retired Admiral Bobby Inman, former Director of NSA, ONI, and Deputy Director of CIA. Remote Viewing work carried out in SAIC was a substantial one.

33. Op. cit. 5, 'The SAIC Era' and 'The Ten Experiments', pp. 3-17, 3-18.

34. Ibid.

35. Previously, the 'Special Branch' of Assistant Deputy Chief of Staff for Operations, Human Intelligence, created in 1979, was specifically used as a vehicle for GRILL FLAME . (Formalization of Project GRILL FLAME. Record released to author 1 February 1996.) But according to a Secret/Eyes Only/Not Releasable to Foreigners teletype, from Major General E.R. Thompson, Assistant Chief of Staff, Intelligence; 'Effective 14 Jan. 81, by approval of Under Secretary of Army, INSCOM [Intelligence Security Command] is now the only active operational GRILL FLAME element in Army.' US Army Intelligence Command record released to author in 1 February 1996.

36. See also 'Former 'Project Stargate' Operative Sets the Record Straight', by Ed Dames, in CE Chronicles, Vol. 4, No. 1, Jan-Feb. 1996, p. 8.

37. For Operation Blue Bird, a see 'Psychic Warned CIA of Attack', the Dallas Morning News, 8 December 1995.

38. For LANDBROKER, see Chapter 8.

39. Paul Smith.

The Mind Controllers

Chapter Eleven

Electronic Implants

Jose Delgado's development of the Stimoceiver in the 1950s – a miniature electrode capable of receiving and transmitting electronic signals by FM radio – brought intelligence agencies' ultimate dream of controlling human behaviour one step closer to reality, because a Stimoceiver could be placed within an individual's cranium. And once in place, an outside operator could manipulate the subject's responses.

In the course of my research I have met people with similar electronic implants in their heads. These devices were placed there without consent. Moreover, the existence of such electronic implants are certified by independent doctors and radiologists. Delgado demonstrated the potential of his Stimoceivers by wiring up a fully-grown bull. With the device in place, Delgado stepped into the ring with the bull. The animal charged towards the experimenter – and then suddenly stopped, just before it reached him. The powerful beast had been stopped with the simple action of pushing a button on a small black box held in Delgado's hand.[1]

In 1966, while reflecting on his research, Delgado asserted that his experiments, 'support the distasteful conclusion that motion, emotion and behaviour can be directed by electrical forces and that humans can be controlled like robots by push buttons.' He went further and suggested there would come a time when brain control could be turned over to non-human operators by establishing two-way radio communication between the implanted brain and a computer.[2]

Since the publication of Delgado's ground-breaking book 'Physical Control of the Mind: Towards a Psychocivilised Society',[3] in which there is a comprehensive account of using implants for the electronic stimulation of the brain (ESB), enormous progress has been made in this particular field.

Delgado, in a series of experiments, made further progress. By attaching a Stimoceiver to the tympanic membrane in the ear, he managed to transform the ear into a kind of microphone. As a result, anything whispered into the ear of a laboratory cat fixed with a Stimoceiver could be heard over a loudspeaker. According to Victor Marchetti, a CIA officer who left the Company both disillusioned and disappointed due to such unethical programmes, the Agency once attempted a highly sophisticated extension of this idea by attaching radio implants to a cat's cochlea, so making the experiment more sensitive, and enabling them to pinpoint specific conversations.[4]

A two page record released by the CIA, amongst several others, dated 19 March 1967, entitled 'Views on Trained Cats (word deleted) for (word deleted) Use' provides some tentative evidence on this subject. In 1923, Bernard Bernardovich Kazhinsky wrote a Russian report entitled A Russian report, 'Biological Radio Communication'. He was an electrical engineer and one of the early researchers in the new area of physio-mathematical sciences. His report captured the attention of the Americans and was translated by the Foreign Technology Division, Air Force Systems Command, Wright-Patteson Air Force Base in Ohio. It explains in detail the same 'cat-spy' concept: 'This book is devoted to examination of a highly interesting problem in modern science: the nature and essence of certain phenomena of electromagnetic communication between living organisms. This subject does not get much attention in world literature, and is the subject of heated arguments and discussions but no common point of view has yet developed in this area. The material outlined in this book ranges from the experiments in mental suggestions to animals, then to people, to the idea of creating a 'thought register', an 'electronic hypnotiser' and 'thought transference over distances.'

This is confirmation the Soviets studied the same concept, decades before Delgado.

Further developments in the design and use of Stimoceivers made their application in humans possible. Ralph Schwitzgebel devised a 'bug-in-the-ear' by which a therapist could communicate with his subject.[5]

The most revealing evidence in hand about the use of Stimoceivers are the records released on the Sub-project 94, part of Project MKULTRA. A memorandum dated 22 November 1961 describes the purpose:

'1. The purpose of this sub-project is to provide a continuation of activities in selected species of animals. Miniaturised stimulating electrode implants in specific brain centre areas will be utilised.

'2. Initial biological work on techniques and brain locations essential to providing conditioning and control of animal has been completed. The feasibility of remote control of activities in several species of animals has been demonstrated.

'The present investigations are directed toward improvement of techniques and will provide a precise mapping of the useful brain centres in selected species. The ultimate objective of this research is to provide an understanding of the mechanisms involved in the directional control of animals and to provide practical systems suitable for (deleted – 'human'?]) application.'

The signatory of this memorandum, Chief – TSD/Research Branch, further adds that 'personnel connected with the planning and monitoring of this programme possess TOP SECRET approval.'

Others were also engaged in researching the use of electronic implants for behavioural control. James Olds,[6] illustrated how areas of the brain near and within the hypothalamus when electronically stimulated would produce 'rewarding' and 'aversive' effects. Robert G. Heath, of Tulane University, achieved great notoriety by implanting 125 electrodes in his subjects, in an attempt to 'cure' homosexuality with ESB. He soon discovered that he could control his patient's memory by inducing fear, arousal, hallucination and pleasure.[7] Heath's accomplishments were based on the work conducted earlier by B.F. Skinner, John C. Lilly, a dolphin researcher, had already accomplished similar effects using devices of his own invention during the 1950s. Using ESB, monkeys continually stimulated themselves to orgasm at three minute intervals for sixteen hours a day.[8]

Brothers Ralph and Robert Schwitzgebel produced a range of devices for tracking individuals over long distances. They were, in this sense, pioneers of what has become known as the 'house arrest concept'. Their bio-sensing devices could be used in monitoring an individual's physical as well as neurological signs within a one mile radius, which showed a great advance on Delgado's earlier work.

After his initial cumbersome brain implants, Ralph Schwitzgebel perfected the technology on a miniaturised scale, and proposed to mount radio receivers on utility poles throughout a targeted area, thereby providing a 24-hour monitoring capability. Although, like Heath, he was keen to use his intracranial implants to 'cure' homosexuality, he was, however, happy to apply his technology to the monitoring of social outcasts and criminals.

Joseph A. Meyer, of the National Security Agency (NSA), took this concept one step further. He suggested the use of electronic implants in almost all Americans who have been arrested – note, arrested, not convicted – for any crime. The 'subscribers' could be monitored continually with computers. He even worked out the necessary budget and economics for his plan, adding that 'subscribers' would 'rent' the implant from the state.[9]

During this period, when many scientists were competing with each other on how to control human behaviour, very few moral objections were presented.

Dr John Lilly (who worked with dolphins and researched into sensory deprivation and drugs) once reminded the director of the National Institute for Mental Health (NIMH – a CIA-funded conduit) of an important dilemma: 'Dr Antoine Remond, using our techniques in Paris, has demonstrated that this method of stimulation of the brain can be applied to the human without the help of a neurosurgeon; he is doing it in his office in Paris without neurosurgical supervision. This means that anyone with the proper apparatus can carry out this on a person covertly, with no external signs that electrodes have been used on that person covertly. I feel that if this technique got into the hands of a security agency, they would have control over a human being and be able to change his beliefs extremely quickly, leaving little evidence of what they had done.'[10] It should be noted that Lilly's own work on monkeys carried a 'secret' classification.

Research into psycho-electronics was extensive. Informants have told me of CIA and military efforts, and projects involving brain implants, microwaves, ESB, and related technologies. In all these efforts, secrecy has always been of the essence.

A file released to me on 21 May 1991 by the office of the Inspector General of Department of the US Army and originally dated 22 August 1975, is a good demonstration of how patients were used as guinea pigs for mind control studies. Electrodes were inserted into parts of their brains, ostensibly because it could help to heal them.

A memorandum to the Inspector General and Auditor General of the Department of the Army says: 'The first important question raised by the Chemical Corps report is whether electrodes were implanted into the brain of the mentally ill subjects for their own good or for the good of 'science'. This would be a complicated question even if all the facts were presented in these reports. In the report dated January 1958, "Correlation of Rhinencephalic Electrograms With

The Mind Controllers

Behavior in Humans", Dr Monroe states simply that it was done, "for therapeutic purposes, namely electro stimulation".'

Alas, details of what occurred are scant and the criteria used to select patients have not been revealed. Some patient case histories however raise ethical questions in the minds of both medical and lay readers. For example, patient A16 in the January 1958 report had two separate operations to implant electrodes, even though it is not clear if she was helped by the first procedure. Whether this was morally justified hangs on whether the operation was performed to help the patient or merely to further medical research.

The 'Results' section from a report on other cases (page 18 of the report) says: 'Any chance for finer correlations between behaviour and electrographic changes was obviated by the type of clinical material with which we are dealing. Most of the patients were chronic, uncooperative, or of low intelligence, hence had little ability for any detailed introspective reporting.'

The appearance of a conflict of interest between investigators and their subjects later led to higher standards being brought in, requiring that an expert physician who was not associated with an experiment should participate in the actual therapeutic decision-making.

The subjects were sometimes operated on and administered with experimental drugs and the rationale for this is not dealt with in the reports. Also, it is not indicated what information the investigators hoped to gain from the experiments. A footnote on page 3 of the January 1958 report suggests that the implantation of electrodes was financed from a grant issued by the 'Commonwealth Foundation'. Judging from the reports, Chemical Corps grant was funding the drug research on patients.

A June 1956 paper on 'Activation of Psychosis with Alpha-Chloralose and Scopolamine Combination' is a case in point, since the express purpose of the study was to try to produce abnormal electroencephalogram tracings in psychiatric and neurological patients. Other drug experiments with mescaline and LSD may have been justified on therapeutic grounds since these drugs were at one time felt by many psychiatrists to be useful in the treatment of mental illness.

Nevertheless, the credulity of many reviewers will be taxed as they read the report on patient known as S.M. in a June 1956 paper. This 27-year-old woman with periodic rage reactions had electrodes implanted and was then administered LSD, Alpha-Chloralose (twice), Frenquil, Mescaline, Metrazol, Alpha-Chloralose plus Amytal, and several other drugs. These tests would be more honestly described as investigations into the basic mechanism of brain pharmacology than as diagnostic or treatment trials. All these studies, according to the file, were conducted, 'within the framework of a 'multidisciplinary research programme' under the overall direction of Robert G. Heath, MD, Chairman of the Department of Neurology and Psychiatry, Tulane University, and Russell R. Monroe, MD, the principle investigator for the Chemical Corps grant. The programme produced a multitude of 'Progressive Reports' such as, 'Correlation and Cortical and Sub-cortical Electrical Recording with Changes in Behaviour During the Administration of d-LSD-25 and Mescaline' (dated 1 April 1955); 'Activation of Psychosis with Alpha-Chloralose and Scopolamine Combination' (dated 1 June 1956); 'Correlation of Rhinencephalic Electrograms with Behavior in Humans' (dated 1 January 1958); and a number of similar reports involving animal experimentation and studies, of which the US Army did not appear to have any objections.

The Mind Controllers

Footnotes:

1. Film footage in author's archive.

2. David Kreech, 'Controlling The Mind Controllers', in THINK 32, July/August 1966.

3. A great part of Delgado's work was funded by the Office of Naval Intelligence. ONI worked very closely with the CIA during the 1950s and 1960s on a wide range of behavioural control programmes.

4. John Ranelagh, 'The Agency, The Rise And Decline Of The CIA', (Sceptre Books, 1988), p. 208.

5. Scheflin and Opton p. 347.

6. L. N. Scheflin and Edward M. Opten, Mind Manipulators, pp 332/7, (Paddington Press 1978).

7. ibid. pp. 332/7.

8. Lilly, p. 90.

9. Scheflin and Opten, pp. 351-55. Meyer uses New York's Harlem as an ideal model community for his mind control hypothesis system.

10. Lilly, p. 91.

Chapter Twelve

The Hypnosis Trials

The CIA has conducted extensive research into the use of hypnosis for defensive and offensive operations. A substantial slice of its resources were allocated to closely monitor the progress made by its international adversaries, especially the Soviets and other communist inspired countries. The picture that emerges is hazy and only recently have we begun to see the far-reaching and disastrous effects this secret work has had on its 'victims'.

The first evidence of the use of hypnosis as an operational tool is found in the work of Morse Allen in 1954. This was at the height of Project ARTICHOKE's attempt to use hypnosis to 'programme' an assassin. John Marks disclosed that around this time, MKULTRA officials, including Gittinger, recommended the use of hypnosis in operational experiments 'on at least one occasion' in 1959.[1]

A CIA report headed 'For Official Use Only' and prepared in 1978 ('Unperceived Manifestations of Mental Processes in Deep Hypnosis') is a translation of a Russian report in 'Voprosy Filosofii', written by V.L. Raykov. This document not only provides a fascinating insight into the subject, but also highlights how international such research had become.

An experimenter called F.J. Evans told his subjects while in deep hypnosis that they would be unable to perceive the number '6' while trying to solve basic mathematical problems when they 'came to'.[2] This experiment introduced a paradoxical philosophical question; must the subjects first perceive the number '6' before they were able to disregard it?

In 1966 the CIA produced a confidential technical report – 'Hypnosis in Intelligence'. 'Most of the proposed uses of hypnosis in intelligence work, partic-

ularly the defensive applications, involve posthypnotic suggestions,' it reported. The Agency had
discovered that 'conservatively, a posthypnotic
suggestion is believed to remain effective for several
months, and beyond this, for years, if periodically reinforced.'[3]

Equally significant was the interest the CIA has paid
to self-hypnosis (also called autosuggestion.) The
hypnotist implanted the belief that thereafter the
subject would be able to hypnotise himself or herself
on a signal the hypnotist provided.

Again, the worry was expressed that rival intelligence services might be more advanced in this area.
The CIA report said: 'The possibility that hypnosis has
been used and even now is being used by oppositional
forces is quite real. There are a number of ways that
hypnosis could be extremely valuable, particularly in
extracting information and co-operation from an otherwise refractory (stubborn) source.'[4]

Clearly showing the potential for exploitation,
hypnosis was used effectively without subjects even
being aware they were being manipulated. There were
three situations: during sleep; on patients undergoing
psychiatric consultation; and spontaneously in individuals observing another subject being hypnotised.

The possibility of hypnosis being misused raises
serious questions about a number of bizarre crimes
and mysterious deaths, and their 'official' explanation.
Examples would be the John F Kennedy assassination;
the suicide of 13 scientists working at the American
Los Alamos National Laboratories; and, similarly, some
who worked at Marconi in the UK. More recently there
have been three deaths at the secret Australian
nuclear research facility at Lucas Heights, New South
Wales. The CIA's own secret report shows that the
Agency was well aware of such possibilities: 'Within
recent years, three documented cases in which hypnosis is said to have played a role in criminal behaviour
have been reported.'[5]

In the case reported by Kroener, a young, sensitive and unmarried male school teacher came under the hypnotic influence of a neighbour. Beginning with neighbourly hospitality, the neighbour built up a relationship where he was able, by hypnotic suggestion, to get the teacher to give or lend him small sums of money and goods. As a test of his power, [the neighbour] then implanted the posthypnotic suggestion that the teacher would shoot himself in the left hand. The teacher did actually shoot himself in the left elbow and was convinced the shooting was an accident. Finally, the hypnotist caused his victim to confess to crimes that he [the neighbour] had committed, and that the teacher had played no part in. Throughout the affair, lasting five years, the teacher had no recollection of the hypnotic sessions. He was convicted on the basis of his posthypnotically induced confession, but through a chance remark began to suspect the nature of his relationship with the neighbour. After many appeals, he was recommended for examination by Kroener, who eventually uncovered the true course of events by re-hypnotising him and causing him to remember the hypnotic experiences with his neighbour.'[6]

The CIA study added that W.R. Wells, a renowned investigator in the area of hypnosis, reported that 'none of his subjects were able to resist a prearranged unacceptable command or indeed any other' which was given to them as a posthypnotic suggestion. 'By posthypnotic suggestion, Wells caused a subject to steal a dollar bill from the hypnotist's coat. The subject was unaware of his action and vigorously denied that he had stolen the money.' Wells argued that 'failure to compel such acts does not disprove the possibility of doing it, whereas even one success demonstrates that it can be done.'

J.M. Schneck and J.G. Watkins, two army officers, produced behaviour, through the use of hypnosis, that ordinarily would be regarded as criminal. Schneck, in his 'A Military Offence Induced by Hypnosis: a case study', inadvertently 'caused a soldier to desert his duty in order to carry out a suggestion for posthypnotic action.' Similarly, J.G. Watkins 'induced a soldier to strike a superior officer by suggesting that the officer was a Japanese soldier.' And he obtained from a hypnotised WAC [member of the Women's Army Corps] 'information classified secret that she had previously told him she would not reveal.'[7]

There are other study reports which confirm that posthypnotic suggestion techniques were used operationally. L.W. Rowland 'asked two deeply hypnotised subjects to pick up a large, active, diamondback rattlesnake. He told them that the snake was a coil of rope. One subject complied immediately, but was prevented from handling the snake by a pane of [almost] invisible glass. The other subject came out of hypnosis and refused to continue the experiment. The next two subjects attempted to grab the snake even when they were told what it was. Similarly, two subjects who were told to throw sulphuric acid at a laboratory assistant (protected by glass) complied with the hypnotist's commands.'[8]

P.C. Young 'replicated Rowland's study, asking eight deeply hypnotised subjects to carry out similar tasks. Seven out of the eight subjects entered into situations that unhypnotised subjects shrank from, that is, they attempted to handle snakes and hurtled acid under conditions from which they themselves recoiled in the waking state.'[9]

In terms of the defensive uses of hypnosis, the CIA on advice given by its professional hypnotists, proposed that 'hypnosis could be used to strengthen the defences of personnel captured or detained by hostile forces.' The agency embarked on a comprehensive study of available data. The success of these studies were mainly related to the employment of 'the astute use of posthypnotic suggestions.'[10] It was known that a subject could be programmed under hypnosis to reject attempts by another hypnotist to induce trances. Such a person would be taught to 'simulate [a] trance or to respond inappropriately whenever he is being used by another hypnotist.'[11]

The US and NATO both used this aspect of autosuggestion; the defensive role included measures to prevent unauthorised hypnosis, and autosuggestion was used to make difficult situations easier to bear. 'With training in autosuggestion, personnel should be able to postpone and temporarily alleviate the disabling effects of long isolation.'[12] By inducing a long period of sleep by the use of autosuggestion, the subject could reduce – or even overcome – their stressful situation. The CIA also carried out research on how to use drugs to reduce the resistance of a subject to hypnosis. 'Almost invariably the drugs used have been depressants, mainly barbiturates. Depressant drugs induce relaxation and relaxation is generally believed to enhance suggestibility.'[13] However, the Agency did not limit its scope merely to the use of LSD and associated drugs. A.M. Weitzenhoffer, in his book 'Hypnotism: An Objective Study in Suggestibility', claimed 'sub-anaesthetic doses of various anaesthetic drugs make subjects more suggestible, provided the subject possesses initially a modicum of suggestibility.'[14]

L.R. Wolberg obtained 'good results with sodium amytal administered slowly, intravenously in sub-anaesthetic doses,' thereby creating a 'feeling of helplessness in the patient while arousing archaic dependency feelings toward the operator.'[15]

An undated report (released on 14 January 1977) entitled 'Hypnosis in Interrogation', said 'control over a person's behavior ostensibly achieved in hypnosis nominates it for use in the difficult process of interrogation.' It asked: 'First, can hypnosis be induced under conditions of interrogation? If so, can the subject be compelled to reveal information? And finally, if information can be so obtained, how reliable will it be?'

The Mind Controllers

The options available were, either to induce a hypnotic trance against the subject's will, or without them being aware of it. In cases where subjects were antagonistic, Wells, Watkins and Bremen obtained some level of success. Subjects making an effort to resist trance induction were usually unable to fight it off.

George H. Easterbrook 'proposed that (hypnosis) might be used to make personnel hypnosis-proof on capture by the enemy, to induce in the subject amnesia for sensitive material in the event of capture, or to help them resist, particularly pain, in captivity.'[16] What is clear is that the agency made extensive use of it in many of their operations. Another key area of CIA research was 'Obedience in a Trance'. To what extent would a subject, appropriately conditioned, be able to retain control over secret information while in a deep trance? It was found that certain types of information given under hypnotic influence to an individual cannot be retrieved, unless the key element (a word, sentence, piece of music, picture, etc.) is given. Like opening a vault, one must have the proper combination for the lock.

P. Janet[17] asked a 'deeply hypnotised female to commit several murders before a distinguished group of judges and magistrates, stabbing some victims with rubber daggers and poisoning others with sugar tablets.'[18] The hypnotised subject did all these things without hesitation. Others, like Watkins and Wells, had already demonstrated this.

The CIA used other methods, such as 'pseudo-hypnosis', (a type of hypnosis administered on targets in the course of a training course without their knowledge) as an interrogation aid. Most of these programmes were derived from psychological warfare techniques. CIA officers used them to train various military personnel (US and NATO) in the use of 'Magic Rooms' or 'Fun Chambers' – either to interrogate subjects or to make friendly forces more resistant to various means of modern interrogation methods. White noise and other forms of sound were used to disorientate subjects and make them more pliant.

Remote hypnosis was also studied. One of the special projects that the CIA has never officially admitted to is the Radio Hypnotic Intercerebral Control (RHIC) project. This involved the use of a Stimoceiver – a micro-miniaturised electronic device (see Chapter 10) to induce a hypnotic state. To activate such a device a subject had to be implanted with one, using an intramuscular technique.

In the early stages of experimentation with this device, surgeons used to leave behind very small scars on the victim's body. In later years, more advanced techniques left no external mark. The nasal cavity and the ear were generally used for implantation. Afterwards, victims often had severe headaches or unexpected nosebleeds.

Former FBI agent, Arthur J. Ford, who left the Bureau to become a journalist under the name of Lincoln Lawrence,[19] was the first to reveal RHIC in his 1965 book 'Were We Controlled?' He describes how it functioned: 'It is the ultra sophisticated application of posthypnotic suggestion triggered at will by radio transmission. It is a recurring hypnotic state, re-induced automatically by the same radio control. An individual is brought under hypnosis. This can be brought into play under many guises. He is then programmed to perform certain actions and maintain certain attitudes upon radio signal.'

The CIA used RHIC extensively in the US and Europe. Canada, another close US ally, also conducted valuable research, which included practical experiments on innocent victims. These experiments were conducted under the close watch of Dr Solandt – the same doctor who approved the secret study of UFO phenomena in Canada, under the code name Project Magnet. Most of this research was concealed in the Department of Transport budget.

The Mind Controllers

The Swedes are believed to be still conducting implantation experiments on unwitting subjects. The original concept for RHIC was, however, conceived by the American military.

Journalist James Moore has claimed to have secured a 350 page manual on RHIC and another project from a CIA source that was prepared in 1963.[20] The manual states: 'Medically, these radio signals are directed to certain parts of the brain. When a part of your brain receives a tiny electrical impulse from outside sources, such as vision, hearing etc., an emotion is produced – anger at the sight of a gang of boys beating an old woman, for example. The same emotion of anger can be created by artificial radio signals sent to your brain by a controller. You could instantly feel the same white hot anger without any apparent reason.'[21]

Dr Jose Delgado, the inventor of the Stimoceiver, wrote: 'radio stimulation of different points in the hymgdala and hippocampus in the four patients produced a variety of effects, including pleasant sensations, elation, deep thoughtful concentration, odd feelings, super relaxation, coloured visions and other responses.'[22] All these effects were achieved by an outside controller. As Delgado stated in 1966, the results of his previous research and experiments 'support the distasteful conclusion that motion, emotion and behaviour can be directed by electronic forces and that humans can be controlled like a robot by push buttons.'[23]

As if that were not bad enough, EDOM – the Electrical Dissolution of Memory – is a refinement of RHIC. It causes 'missing time' or the partial erasure of a subject's memory. This is achieved by the simple blocking, or electronic 'jamming', of some of the brain's synapses through a surfeit of acetocholine. This chemical can stop the neural transmission along certain selected pathways. Besides this chemical technique, both electromagnetism and microwaves can be used to achieve 'missing time'. And, EDOM could also be used as a vehicle for the remote induction of a hypnotic trance.

Lincoln Lawrence's CIA source revealed some frightening information about EDOM: 'there is already in use a small EDOM generator-transmitter, which can be concealed on the body of a person. Contact with this person – a casual handshake or even just a touch – transmits a tiny electronic charge plus an ultra-sonic signal tone which, for a short while, will disturb the time orientation of the person affected.'[24]

These methods (RHIC and EDOM) could deliver suggestions to a subject or erase memory of any act the subject was asked to perform. This was achieved with certain key words (or a series of simple acts) that triggered 'Command-Orders' planted in the memory. The Command-Orders were designed so that, irrespective of how intelligent the subject was, the validity or the logic of a directive was never questioned. The subject blindly carried it through heedless of any danger.

According to a CIA source, the subject could also carry out orders for his or her personal destruction. This was usually done at the completion of a mission for which the subject was initially programmed. If, however, for any reason, the subject becomes a liability, the 'self-destruction' mechanism could be triggered before the completion of the main task. The method, if planned and conducted professionally, would leave behind no clue for enemy investigators.

Footnotes:

1. Marks, John, 'The Search for the Manchurian Candidate', Times Books, 1979, pp 182-192.

2. Evans, F.J. and Thorn, W.F., 'Two Types of Posthypnotic Amnesia: Recall Amnesia and Source Amnesia', International Journal Of Experimental Hypnosis, Vol. 14, 1966, pp 162-179.

3. Hypnosis in Intelligence – Technical Report (Confidential –

CIA), October 1966.

4. ibid.

5. ibid.

6. Orne, M.T., 'The Potential Uses of Hypnosis in Interrogation'. In Biderman, A. and Zimmer, H. (eds.) 'The Manipulation of Human Behaviour', (New York; John Wiley and Sons Inc., 1961).

7. Fisher, S. 'An Investigation of Alleged Conditioning Phenomena Under Hypnosis'. Journal of Clinical Experimental Hypnosis, 1955, 3, pp. 71-103.

8. Rowland, L.W., 'Will Hypnotised Persons Try To Harm Themselves Or Others?' Journal of Abnormal Social Psychology, 1939, 34, pp 114-117.

9. Young, P.C., 'Antisocial Uses of Hypnosis'. In LeCron, L.M. (ed.), 'Experimental Hypnosis'. New York; Macmillan, 1952.

10. See note 7.

11. ibid.

12. ibid.

13. ibid.

14. Weitzenhoffer, A.M., 'Hypnotism: An Objective Study in Suggestibility', (New York; John Wiley and Sons, Inc., 1953).

15. Wolberg, L.R., 'The Principles of Hypnotherapy', Vol. 1, (New York; Crune and Stratton, 1948).

16. Easterbrooks, G.H., 'Hypnotism', (New York; Appleton-Century-Crofts, 1933).

17. Janet, P. 'Psychological Healing; A Historical and Clinical Study', (London; George Allen and Unwin, 1925).

18. ibid.

19. Lawrence's real name was given to me by more than one source as Arthur J. Ford.

20. Bowart, Walter. 'Operation Mindcontrol', (Dell Publishing Co., Inc.), 1978. pp 261-264.

21. ibid., p 263.

22. Delgado, J.M.R., 'Intercerebral Radio Stimulation and Recording in Completely Free Patients', in Schwitzgebel and Schwitzgebel (eds.).

23. Kreech, David. 'Controlling the Mindcontrollers', in Think 32, July/August 1966.

24. Lawrence, Lincoln, 'Were We Controlled?' (University Books, New York; 1965).

The Mind Controllers

Chapter Thirteen

Neural Manipulation

In the 1960s, the US Embassy in Moscow fell under attack from a microwave beam, targeted at the building by the Soviets. This beam was used with the aim of controlling the minds and actions of those within the embassy. The discovery that the Communists were attempting such a sinister form of neural manipulation prompted an urgent inquiry in the US and what follows draws from declassified records on Operation Pandora (see later) released to me on 19 December 1994 after a Freedom of Information Act appeal filed in 1991. Pandora was the US reaction to the events uncovered in Moscow.

In 1961, Allan H. Frey provided evidence that the perception of sound can be induced in hearing as well as deaf humans by irradiating the head with low-power density, pulse-modulated, UHF (ultra high frequency) electromagnetic energy; a type of radio wave. It had previously been shown that the UHF energy of wavelengths smaller than 10cm could produce a heating of the skin which could cause severe burning.

Since then, work by Frey and others has shown that this same microwave energy is capable of producing selective tachy-cardia (a speeding up of the heartbeat) and brachycardia (a slowing down of the heartbeat). In 1973, S.M. Bawin *et al.,* provided further evidence that brain waves can be inhibited or enhanced by low power VHF (very low frequency) energy.[1]

Studies have repeatedly shown since the 1950s that behaviour can be modified with auditory-cortex stimuli, peripheral heating, brain rhythm modification and many other biological applications of microwaves. The energy in question is used in radar which is capable of detecting a single insect at a distance of over 1 kilometre and at an altitude of 600 metres. It is therefore possible that radar-type energy could be used as a weapon focusing either on an individual or on a mass of people.[2]

Although the use of electromagnetic (EM) energy in bio-sciences is considered to be a relatively recent development, bio-electric research dates back at least as far as 1786 when Galvani and Volta were arguing about electricity stimulating frogs' legs. It was not until 1908 that the term 'diathermy' for the heating of body tissues by high frequency current was coined by Von Zeyneck, the pioneer in the use of direct electrodes.[3]

But real progress was made in the 1920s when F. Cazzamali, an Italian physician, discovered that he could induce hallucinations in the minds of highly suggestible individuals, and claimed to have detected radiation from the mind. His work, 'Radiating Brain', was translated in 1965 by the Foreign Technology Division of the Wright-Patterson Air Force in the United States. The Dutch physician, W.A.G. van Everdingen made further progress during 1938-43. He observed that microwave irradiation affected the heart action of the chicken embryo in relation to its glycogen (a form of protein) level.[4]

In 1946, J.E. Nyrop recorded specific effects on bacteria, viruses and tissue cultures of exposure to short-pulsed EM radiation with the heating effect deleted.[5] These early pioneers in biological manipulation with EM energy paved the way for a new era of more detailed research. But it was not until 1961 that the work of Dr Alan H. Frey convinced the scientific community that radio-frequency (RF) energy could indeed do more than heat a tissue culture.

The Pandora files also make reference to work on the direct stimulation of the brain with electrodes. There was interest in how a reaction could be artificially produced, dependent upon the region stimulated. Walter Hess, a Swiss physiologist and Nobel Prize winner, was the first to pioneer the implantation of electrical wires in animal brains in order to record electrical activities. He found that the hypothalamus and associated neural structures located in the rim of the brain stem, the limbic system, controlled emotional and aggressive behaviour.[6] It was also the site of appetite, and sexual behaviour, tied to the sense of smell.

W. Penfield, a neurosurgeon, took Hess' findings one step further. He used electric currents to stimulate the cortex of his patients' brains while the brains were exposed during surgery. The results were astounding. Epileptic patients would re-experience complete episodes from their past. They were so real that it was as if they were literally re-living them. If the same spot was stimulated twice, the entire sequence would repeat itself from the beginning.[7]

In 1960, Neider and Neff used direct electrical stimulation of the brain (ESB) to produce auditory sensations in cats for the purposes of conditioning.[8] They pointed out that sounds are produced by ESB, that sounds are a proven behavioural conditioning stimulus, and that the quality of the sound improves in proportion to the depth of the electrical stimulus in the cerebral cortex.

Radiesthesia is a term for the ability of humans to detect electromagnetic energy. James Beal of NASA's Space Flight Centre, who studies the phenomenon, believes that we are all able to tune in. He believes that external energy may have profound effects due to the fact that each cell, or neuron, is a tiny complex electrical system.[9]

Robert O. Becker, a research orthopaedic surgeon at the State University of New York, suggests that each neuron has the characteristics of a semi-conductor. He believes that the gial cells of the nervous system may actually act as a liquid crystal in resonance with surrounding energy fields.

If this is true, the nervous system is capable of magnifying electrical effects over a million times. Becker is convinced that the brain contains a middle structure with a stronger direct-current field than the rest of the nervous system. The intensity and perhaps the polarity of this current directly influences consciousness. Animals' brainwave patterns went from waking to comatose when Becker placed a magnetic field at the right angle to the brainstem. He then reversed the process. Becker applied direct current to the frontal region of the brain and awoke chemically anaesthetised animals.[10]

Allan H. Frey made the following surprising announcement on 24 April 1961 at an Aerospace Medical Association Meeting in Chicago: 'Our data to date indicates that the human auditory system can respond to electromagnetic energy in at least a portion of the radio frequency (RF) spectrum. Furthermore, this response is instantaneous and occurs at low power densities – densities which are well below that necessary for biological damage.'[11]

Frey placed his subjects over 100 feet from a sweep antenna, which they could not see. There was no sound from the antenna. Yet they reported hearing a buzzing, knocking sound each time the RF beam swept past them. The perceived noise level was estimated at 70 to 80 decibels (db), and earplugs allowed the subjects to hear the sound more clearly. The sounds were the same in all cases, and always seemed to indicate a noise just behind the head. Shielding studies showed that the temple areas were critical to RF sounds. When the temples were shielded the RF sound was gone. There was no doubt that the responses were independent of the tympanic membrane of the ear.

A new form of communications, with immense implications for the military, had been discovered: direct communication to the brain by radio waves. By 1961, experiments had proved that the effect and range of auditory response to RF energy could reach thousands of feet.

With appropriate modulation of the carrier transmitter, the RF energy could create various biological effects on a targeted subject, including 'pins and needles', dizziness, nausea, and vomiting.

The path had been cleared to replace the electrical stimulation of the brain (ESB) using electrodes with RF energy. It was now possible to achieve results similar to those achieved with ESB using radio waves.This discovery makes the creation of a Manchurian Candidate more of a reality. Pulse-modulated transmitters could carry information inserted on the signal. It could even be modulated to send words to the brain.

An expendable intelligence 'asset', programmed by remote hypnosis and then in a post-hypnotic state could be activated by these means, to carry out orders, by-passing their consciousness. Any hypnotic command the target obeyed would be accepted as the target's own idea, apparently originating within his or her brain. A 'timed hypnotic command' could also be given, RF programming being used to trigger a command at a pre-determined time in the future. Similarly, a hypnotic suggestion could be triggered by a word, a picture or other signal.

It was known that brain waves carry data for the processing of information in the brain. W.R. Adey believed that this data was digitally coded using frequency modulation of the waves.[12] If so, it was believed there should be no fundamental difficulty in transmitting brain waves into another person.

J.F. Schapitz suggested to the US State Department the following experiment. 'Brain waves that have been produced by drugs of known psychic effect are going to be registered on magnetic tape. The recorded rhythms will then be modulated onto a microwave (or several beams if there have been multiple tracings) and will thus be transmitted into the brain of non-drugged subjects. Their state of mind will subsequently be investigated by interview, psychological tests and by polygraph recordings. Thus it will be determined whether non-drugged subjects are in the same state of mind as the drugged subjects.' He even proposed to use similar microwave transmission methods to send the muscle movements of an individual to another targeted individual.

It was felt there were also ways of blocking the retrieval of information. By inducing amnesia in a person it would be possible to disrupt, block, inhibit and reconnect his or her conscious (mental) concatenations at will.[13] The social and political implications of this are obviously disturbing. The radio wave energy used in most of the experiments was pulse-modulated or CW (carrier wave) microwaves – as used in radar. Indeed 10cm wavelength radar equipment was used in almost all of these experiments.[14]

Symptoms of microwave irradiation, as used in Operation Pandora, are extreme fatigue, constant or periodic headaches, irritability, sleep disruption, memory difficulties, pains in the region of the heart intensifying after physical stress, laboured respiration, decreased appetite, enlargement of the heart, and other heart problems.[15] A US State Department report by G.W. Biles suggested it was possible to induce a heart attack in a person from a distance with radar, since radar uses the same pulse-modulated wave energy that Frey had used in some of his experiments on isolated frog hearts.[16]

By 1974, Lawrence Pinneo, a neurophysiologist and electronic engineer at Stanford Research Institute in Melano Park, California, had developed a computer system capable of reading a person's mind by correlating the brain waves of subjects on an electroencephalograph with specific commands. Nowadays it is possible to reverse the process using advanced ESB radio techniques.[17] The concept of mind-reading computers is no longer science fiction. Neither is their use by Big Brotherly governments. Major Edward Dames of Psi-Tech said in April 1995 on NBC's 'The Other Side' programme: 'The US Government has an electronic device which could implant thoughts in people.' Dames would not comment any further.

Footnotes:

1. Bawin, S.M., Gavlas-Medici, R.J., and Adey, W.R., Effects of Modulated VHF fields on specific brain rhythms in cats', in 'Brain Research', Vol. 58, 1973, pp. 365-384.

2. 'Microwave US-USSR', Vol. VI, July-December 1976, p. 4, Office of Security, US Department of State.

3. Jaski, Tom and Susskind, Charles, 'Electromagnetic radiation as a tool in the life sciences', in 'Science', vol. 133, no. 3451, 1961, pp. 443-447

4. Ibid.

5. Ibid.

6. Edson, Lee, 'The psyche and the surgeon', in New York Times Magazine, 30 September 1973.

7. Steven, Leonard A., 'Neurons: building blocks of the brain', (Crowell, New York, 1974).

8. Neider, Philip C, and Neff, William D., 'Auditory information from subcortical electrical stimulation in cats', in 'Science' vol. 133, 1961, pp. 1010-1011. They summarised the auditory responses at the beginning of their paper: 'It has long been known that auditory sensations may be produced in human subjects by direct electrical stimulation in or near auditory areas of the cerebral cortex. The sensory effects produced: knocking, booming, buzzing and so on. Some evidence has also come from conditioning studies on animals, in which direct electrical stimulation of areas of the cerebral cortex has been successfully used as the condition stimuli.'

9. Ferguson, Marilyn, 'The Brain Revolution: the frontiers of mind research', Davis-Poynter, (London, 1974).

10. Telephone conversation with the author, May 1992.

11. Allan H. Frey, 'Auditory system response to radio frequency energy', Technical Note in 'Aerospace Medicine', vol. 32, 1961, pp. 1140-1142.

12. Adey, W. R., 'Information storage and recall' in Corning, W.C.

and Balaban, M., 'The Mind: biological approaches to its function', 1968

13. Shapitz, J. F., 'Experimental investigation of effectiveness of psycho-physiological manipulation using modulated electromagnetic energy for direct information transmission into the brain', January 1974: personal unpublished papers submitted to the US State Department.

14. Richter, Juergen H. et al, 'Remote radar sensing: atmospheric structure and insects in 'Science', vol. 180, no 4091, pp. 1176-78.

15. 'Microwave US-USSR', Vol II 1972-1974, US Department of State Office of Security, 'A study of electromagnetic-biological effects', p. 5.

16. 'Microwave US-USSR' 2, p. 4

17. 'Mind reading computer', in Time, July 1, 1974, p. 67. See also David M. Rorvik, 'As Man Becomes Machine', (Sphere Books, London, 1979).

Chapter Fourteen

Non-lethal Weaponry

On 22 April 1993, the main evening news on BBC Television broadcast a story on a new American development – a non-lethal weapon. David Shukman, Defence Correspondent, interviewed (Retired) US Army Colonel John B. Alexander and Janet Morris, two of the main proponents of a concept of disorientating an enemy and rendering them incapable of retaliating without actually causing any obvious physical harm.[1]

Non-lethal weaponry is not new. Devices to disrupt and disturb the enemy have long been used by the intelligence services, police and defence establishments. During the women's protest at Greenham Common military base in Berkshire, the US military used what it termed 'Novel Effect Weapons' such as microwaves against the protesters.[2]

Non-lethal devices have a wide-range of functions – from disrupting the operation of equipment, vehicles or buildings to demoralising and confusing personnel. In December 1980 John Alexander published an article called 'The New Mental Battlefield' in the US Army's journal, Military Review. It referred to claims that telepathy could be used to interfere with the brain's electrical activity. This caught the attention of senior Army generals who encouraged him to pursue what they termed 'soft option kill' technologies and a new way of waging war was therefore born. After retiring from the Army in 1988, Alexander joined the Los Alamos National Laboratories and began working with Janet Morris, the Research Director of the US Global Strategy Council (USGSC), chaired by Dr Ray Cline, former Deputy Director of the CIA.[3] Not surprisingly the Council began to take an interest in the military possibilities of variety of research projects.

The Mind Controllers

Throughout 1990 the USGSC canvassed the main national laboratories, the major defence contractors and industries, retired senior military, and intelligence officers. Supported by Senator Sam Nunn, chair of the Senate Armed Services Committee, a Non-lethality Policy Review Group, was set up led by Major General Chris S. Adams, USAF (retired), former Chief of Staff, Strategic Air Command.[4]

In 1991 Janet Morris issued a number of papers[5] and the US Army Training and Doctrine Command at Fort Monroe, VA, published a detailed draft report on an 'Operations Concept for Disabling Measures'. It included over twenty projects in which Alexander was involved at the Los Alamos National Laboratories.

In a memo dated 10 April 1991, entitled 'Do we need a Non-lethal Defense Initiative?', Paul Wolfwitz, Under Secretary of Defense for Policy, wrote to Defense Secretary Dick Cheney. 'A US lead in non-lethal technologies will increase our options and reinforce our position in the post-Cold War world,' he said, 'Our research and development efforts must be increased.'

Morris was now arguing that while 'war will always be terrible, a world power deserving its reputation for humane action should pioneer the principles of non-lethal defense.'[6] In defining such a strategy', she justified the expenditure of tax dollars on the basis that a doctrine was needed for the use of non-lethal weapons by the US in a crisis 'at home or abroad in a life-serving fashion.'

Little attention was focused on offensive application of the weapons in question, or their misuse, should they become available to 'rogue' nations. Morris said non-lethal weapons would serve the country's interests 'at home and abroad by projecting power without indiscriminately taking lives or destroying property.'[7] She also admitted that 'casualties cannot be avoided.'[8]

According to her thesis, the areas where non-lethal weapons could be useful were 'regional and low intensity conflict (adventurism, insurgency, ethnic violence, terrorism, narco-trafficking, domestic crime).'[9] She believed that 'by identifying tactics and strategic planning' the US could reshape its military capability 'to meet the already identifiable threats' that they might face in a multipolar world 'where American interests are globalised and American presence widespread.'[10]

Morris's paper recommended 'two types of life-conserving technology.' 'Anti-material' techniques for disabling the enemy's infrastructure were listed. One technique would be to destroy or impair the enemy's electronic systems, or in other ways stop mechanical systems from functioning. This could be achieved using:

• Chemical and biological weapons using anti-material agents 'which do not significantly endanger life or the environment, or anti-personnel agents which have no permanent effects.'[11]

• Laser blinding systems to incapacitate the electronic sensors, or optics, i.e. light detection and ranging. Already the Army Infantry School was developing a one-man portable laser weapon system known as the Infantry Self-Defense System. (The US Army's Armament Research, Development and Engineering Center (ARDEC), was also engaged in the development of non-lethal weapons under their programme called 'Low Collateral Damage Munitions' (LCDM). The LCDM is trying to develop technologies leading to weapons capable of dazzling and incapacitating missiles, armoured vehicles and personnel.)

• Non-lethal electromagnetic technologies.

• Non-nuclear electromagnetic pulse weapons.[12] General Norman Schwartzkopf, head of allied forces in the Gulf War, told the US Joint Chiefs of Staff that one such weapon stationed in space with a 'wide-area-pulse capacity' had the ability to fry enemy electronics. What is less known is the fate of enemy personnel in such a scenario. In a joint project with the Los Alamos National Laboratories and with technical support from the US Army's Harry Diamond

Laboratories, ARDEC was developing High Power Microwave (HPM) 'projectiles'. According to ARDEC, the Diamond lab had already 'completed a radio frequency effects analysis on a representative target set' for (HPM).

• Among the chemical agents, so-called 'supercaustics', 'millions of times more caustic than hydrofluoric acid,'[13] were prime candidates. An artillery round could deliver jellied super-acids which could destroy the optics/glass of a heavily armoured vehicles and 'could be used to silently destroy key weapons systems.'[14] Also mentioned by Morris are net-like entanglements to delay vehicles, or 'stealthy' metal boats with a low radar signature 'for night actions, or any seaborne or come-ashore stealthy scenario.'[15] Another seemingly bizarre way of targeting enemy equipment at a distance was the use of 'chemical or liquid metal embrittlement' and 'anti-material polymers.' These would be used with aerosol dispersal systems to spread chemical adhesives or lubricants (using Teflon).

The second category revealed by the documents are 'anti-personnel non-lethal technologies':

• Hand-held lasers which are meant 'to dazzle', but which could also cause the eyeball to explode and to blind the target.

• Isotropic radiators, that is explosively driven munitions capable of generating very bright omnidirectional light, with similar effects to laser guns.

• High-power microwaves (HPM) as mentioned above. US Special Operations Command already had that capability within their grasp as a portable microwave weapon.[16] As Myron L. Wolbarsht, a Duke University opthalamist and expert in laser weapons stated: 'US Special Forces can quietly cut enemy communications but also can cook internal organs.'[17]

• Another candidate was 'Infrasound' using acoustic beams. In conjunction with the Scientific Applications and Research Associates (SARA) of Huntingdon,

California, ARDEC and Los Alamos laboratories were busy 'developing a high power, very low frequency acoustic beam weapon.' They were also looking into methods of projecting non-diffracting (i.e. non-penetrating) high frequency acoustic bullets. Already some governments have used infrasound as a means of crowd control, for example in France. ARDEC scientists were looking further into methods of using pulsed chemical lasers. These could project 'a hot, high pressure plasma in the air in front of a target surface, creating a blast wave that will result in variable but controlled effects on material and personnel.'

• Very low frequency (VLF) sound (20-35 KHz), or low-frequency RF modulations can cause nausea, vomiting and abdominal pains. 'Some very low frequency sound generators, in certain frequency ranges, can cause the disruption of human organs and, at high power levels, can crumble masonry.'[18]

The CIA had a similar programme in 1978 called Operation Pique, which included the bouncing of radio or microwave signals off the ionosphere, apparently to affect the mental functions of people in target areas, including Eastern European nuclear installations.[19]

The entire non-lethal weapon concept is literally a Pandora's Box of unknown consequences. The main person behind this concept was Col. Alexander. Born in New York in 1937, he spent part of his career as a Commander of Green Berets Special Forces in Vietnam, led Cambodian mercenaries behind enemy lines, and took part in a number of clandestine programmes, including Operaton Phoenix. He currently holds the post of Director of Non-lethal Programs at Los Alamos National Laboratories. In 1980 he was awarded a PhD from Walden University[20] and has long been interested in fringe topics. In 1971, while a captain in the infantry at Schofield Barracks, Honolulu, he dived off the Bemini Islands looking for the lost continent of Atlantis. He was an official representative for the Silva mind control organisation, which holds courses all over the world, and a lecturer on 'Precataclysmic Civilisations'.[21] Alexander is also a past President and a Board member of the International Association for Near Death Studies; and, with his former wife, Jan Northup, he helped Dr C.B. Scott Jones perform ESP experiments with dolphins.[22]

Retired Major General Albert N. Stubblebine (Former Director of US Army Intelligence and Security Command) and Alexander are on the board of a 'remote viewing' company called Psi-Tech. The company also employs Major Edward Dames (ex-Defence Intelligence Agency), Major David Morehouse (ex-82nd Airborne Division), and Ron Blackburn (former microwave scientist and specialist at Kirkland Air Force Base). Psi-Tech has received several government contracts. For example, during the Gulf War crisis the Department of Defense asked it to use remote viewing to locate Saddam's Scud missiles sites. In 1992 the FBI sought Psi-Tech's assistance to locate a kidnapped Exxon executive.[23]

With Major Richard Groller and Janet Morris as his co-authors, Alexander published 'The Warrior's Edge' in 1990.[24] The book describes in detail various unconventional methods which would enable the practitioner to acquire 'human excellence and optimum performance' and thereby become an 'invincible warrior.'[25] The stated purpose of the book is 'to unlock the door to the extraordinary human potentials inherent in each of us. To do this, we, like governments around the world, must take a fresh look at non-traditional methods of affecting reality. We must raise human consciousness of the potential power of the individual body/mind system – the power to manipulate reality. We must be willing to retake control of our past, present, and ultimately, our future.'[26]

Alexander is a friend of Clinton's Vice President Al Gore, their relationship dating back to 1983 when Gore was in Alexander's Neuro-Linguistic Programming (NLP). Released documentation shows that NLP 'presented to selected general officers and Senior Executive Service members'[27] a set of techniques to modify behaviour patterns.[28] Among the first generals to take the course was Lieutenant General Maxwell Thurman, who later went on to receive his fourth star and become Vice-Chief of Staff at the Army and Commander Southern Command.[29] Among other senior participants were Tom Downey and Stubblebine.

One of Alexander's pet programmes in 1983 was the Jedi Project, coined from the film Star Wars.[30] In typically abstruse jargon its aim was to seek and 'construct teachable models of behaviorable/ physical excellence using unconventional means.'[31] According to Alexander, it developed from work on Neuro-Linguistic Programming. With the help of friends such as Stubblebine, who was then head of the US Army Intelligence and Security Command, he managed to fund Jedi. In reality the concept was not as new as Alexander tried to portray.

The original idea, which was to show how, using NLP skills, 'human will-power and human concentration affect performance more than any other single factor'[32] was the brainchild of three independent people; Fritz Erikson, a Gestalt therapist, Virginia Satir, a family therapist and Erick Erikson, a hypnotist.

Janet Morris, co-author of The Warrior's Edge, is another noted expert in this area. As well as being research director of USGSC, she is best known as a science fiction writer and has been a member of the New York Academy of Sciences since 1980 as well as a member of the Association for Electronic Defense. Morris was initiated into the Japanese art of bioenergetics, Joh-re, the Indonesian brotherhood of Subud, and graduated from the Silva course in advanced mind control.

She has been conducting remote viewing experiments for fifteen years and worked on a research project investigating the effects of the mind on computer systems.

Morris described to me[33] how Alexander had a close involvement in mind control and psychotronic projects at Los Alamos National Laboratories. He and his team were working with Dr Igor Smirnov, a psychologist from the Moscow Institute of Psychocorrelations. They were invited to the US after Morris paid a visit to Russia in 1991 where she was shown techniques pioneered by the Russian Department of Psycho-Correction at Moscow Medical Academy.

The Russians claimed to be able to analyse the human mind electronically in order to influence it externally. They then transmitted subliminal command messages, using key words in 'white noise' or music.[34] Using an infrasound very low frequency-type transmission, the acoustic psycho-correction message was transmitted via bone conduction. Ear-plugs had no effect on blocking the sound. According to the Russians the subliminal messages by-passed the conscious level and were effective almost immediately.

C.B. Scott Jones, a former assistant to Senator Clairborne Pell (Democrat, Rhode Island), was a member of US Naval Intelligence for 15 years, as well as Assistant Naval Attaché, New Delhi, India, in the 1960s. Jones has briefed the President's Scientific Advisory Committee, and has testified before House and Senate Committees on intelligence matters. After the Navy he 'worked in the private sector research and development community involved in US Government sponsored projects for the Defense Nuclear Agency (DNA), Defense Intelligence Agency (DIA) and US Army Intelligence and Security Command.' He has been head of the Rockefeller Foundations for some time and chairs the American Society for Psychical Research.[35]

Jones is a member of the AVIARY, a shadowy group of intelligence and Department of Defense officers and scientists with a brief to discredit any serious research in the UFO field. Each member of the AVIARY bears a bird's name. Jones is FALCON.

One of their agents was UFO researcher William Moore who was introduced to John Alexander at a party in 1987 by Scott Jones. Moore told an audience at a conference held by the Mutual UFO Network (MUFON) on 1 July 1989 in Las Vegas that he was promised inside information by the senior members of AVIARY in return for his 'obedience' and assistance. He helped to propagate and disseminate disinformation fed to him by various members and said he was instructed to target Dr Paul Bennewitz, an electronics expert.

The doctor had accumulated some UFO film footage and recordings of electronic signals of unexplained events in 1980 over the Menzano Weapons Storage areas, at Kirtland Air Force Base, New Mexico. As a result of AVIARY's attack, coupled with surreptitious break-ins and mental pressure, Bennewitz ended up in a psychiatric hospital.

A few years ago, before I unmasked two members of AVIARY,[36] I was visited by two others (MORNING DOVE and HAWK) who had travelled to the UK with a message from the senior ranks advising me not to go ahead with my exposé. I rejected this proposal. Immediately after publication, Alexander confessed he was indeed a member, nicknamed PENGUIN. The accuracy of my information was further confirmed by yet another member, Ron Pandolphi, known as PELICAN. He has a physics doctorate and works at the Rocket and Missile section of the Office of the Deputy Director of Science and Technology, CIA. The role of Alexander is therefore ambiguous, though a noted expert in non-lethal weapons he appears keen to divert attention from the more sensitive work of his collaborators.

In his book, 'Out There',[37] the New York Times journalist Howard Blum refers to 'a UFO Working Group' within the Defense Intelligence Agency. Despite DIA's repeated denials,[38] the existence of this working group has been confirmed to me by more than one member of the group itself, including an independent source in the Office of Naval Intelligence.

The majority of the group are senior members of the AVIARY: Dr Christopher Green (BLUEJAY) being from the CIA;[39] Harold Puthoff (OWL) ex-NSA; Dr Jack Verona (RAVEN) (DoD was one of the initiators of the DIA's Sleeping Beauty project which aimed to achieve battle-field superiority using mind-altering electromagnetic weaponry).

Alexander's position as the Programme Manager for 'Contingency Missions of Conventional Defense Technology', Los Alamos National Laboratories, gave him a lot of power. One of his interests was the Department of Defense's Project RELIANCE 'which encourages a search for all possible sources of existing and incipient technologies before developing new technology in-house.'[40] Sometimes defence contractors like McDonnel Douglas Aerospace were involved.

I have several reports, some of which were compiled before his arrival at Los Alamos when he was with Army Intelligence, which show Alexander's keen interest in any and every exotic subject – UFOs, ESP, psychotronics, anti-gravity devices, near death experiments, psychology warfare and non-lethal weaponry.

John Alexander utilises the bank of information he has accumulated to try to develop psychotronic, psychological and mind weaponry. He began thinking about non-lethal weapons a decade ago in his paper 'The New Mental Battlefield'. He seems to want to become a 'Master.' If he ever succeeds in this ambition the rest of us ordinary mortals had better watch out.

Footnotes:

1. Letter dated 2 April 1993, to author from Mrs Victoria Alexander.

2. The intimidation was carried out by the US Army Chemical and Military Police.

3. The United States Global Strategy Council is an independent

think tank, incorporated in 1981. It focuses on long-range strate-
gic issues. The founding members were Clare Boothe Luce,
General Maxwell Taylor, General Albert Wedemeyer, Dr Ray Cline
(Co-chair), Jeane Kirkpatrick (Co-chair), Morris Leibman, Henry
Luce III, J. William Middendorf II, Admiral Thomas H. Moorer
USN (retd), General Richard Stilwell (retd.), Dr Michael A.
Daniles (President), Dr Dalton A. West (Executive Vice
President). Its Research Directors were Dr Yonah Alexander, Dr
Roger Fontaine, Robert L. Katula and Janet Morris.

4. Nonlethality: Development of a National Policy and employing
Nonlethal Means in a New Strategic Era – a Project of the US
Global Strategy Council, 1991, p. 4. Other staff members at the
USGSC are Steve Trevino, Dr John B. Alexander and Chris Morris.

5. The USGSC has issued a wide variety of papers on the
Nonlethal Weapons Concept. For example, 'In Search of
Nonlethal Strategy', (Janet Morris); 'Nonlethality: A Global
Strategy – White Paper'; 'Nonlethality Briefing Supplement No. 1';
and 'Nonlethality in the Operational Continuum'.

6. 'In Search of a Nonlethal Strategy', Janet Morris, p. 1.

7. 'Nonlethality: a Global Strategy – White Paper', p. 3.

8. 'In Search of a Nonlethal Strategy', Janet Morris, p. 3.

9. In the recent cult siege in Waco, Texas, a 'nonlethal' technique,
projecting subliminal messages, was used to influence David
Kuresh – without success.

10. 'Nonlethality: a Global Strategy – White Paper', p. 2.

11. The computer data base compiled during the CIA/Army's
Project OFTEN, examining several thousand chemical
compounds, during 1976-1973, is a most likely candidate for any
chemical agents for non-lethal weapons.

12. The British MoD is already developing a 'microwave bomb'.
Work on the weapon is going on at the Defence Research Agency
at Farnborough, Hampshire. See Sunday Telegraph 27 September
1992, partly reproduced in Lobster 24, p. 14. The Royal Navy is
already in possession of laser weapons which dazzle aircraft
pilots. The Red Cross has called for them to be banned under
the Geneva Convention because could permanently blind. In

The Mind Controllers

1997, the Technical Advisor to the International Committee of the Red Cross, Dominique Loye met with me to discuss relevant issues concerning non-lethal weapons, and how ICRC could be of influence in banning their use. In December 1998, he issued a White Paper 'Non-Lethal' Weapons and International Humanitarian Law, expressing ICRC's serious concern concerning the use of these weapons. In his final remarks he writes: In conclusion, having examined the literature on 'non-lethal' weapons in the light of the law of war, we are prompted to stress the following;

· The term 'non-lethal' is misleading.

· The law of war is directly relevant to 'non-lethal' technologies, i.e. the rules of the law of war applicable to weapons must be applied to each new weapon, including 'non-lethal' weapons';

· To discuss any 'non-lethal' weapon in the light of the law of war, it is necessary and urgent to better understand the possible effects on humans of the proposed weapon;

· The legality of combining the effects of certain 'non-lethal' weapons with those of existing conventional weapons needs to be carefully examined.

13. 'In Search of a Nonlethal Strategy', Janet Morris, p. 13.

14. ibid.

15. Then US Navy, through its Project SEA SHADOW, has already developed a stealth boat. Like the Lockheed F117A, stealth fighter, it leaves no radar signature – BBC, Newsround, 28 April 1993.

16. Taped conversation with Janet Morris, 1 March 1993.

17. The Wall Street Journal, 4 January 1993.

18. In Search of a Non-lethal Strategy, p. 14.

19. Remote Control Technology, Anna Keeler (Full Disclosure, Ann Arbor, USA, 1989) p.11.

20. Walden University, 801 Anchor Road Drive, Naples, Fl. 33904, USA. Walden University considers itself a non-traditional university and does not offer any undergraduate courses to its students.

21.Brad Steiger, Mysteries of Space and Time, (Prentice Hall, Englewood Cliffs, New Jersey) pp. 72 – 73.

The US Army Command and General College, Fort Leavenworth, Kansas, issued this on Alexander's career: 'Colonel John. B. Alexander, US Army Retired, manages Antimateriel Technology at Los Alamos National Laboratories, Los Alamos, New Mexico. His military assignments included; Advanced Systems Concepts Office, Laboratory Command; manager, Technology Integration Office, Army Material Command; assistant deputy chief of staff, Technology Planning and Management, Army Material Command; and chief, Advanced Human Technology, Intelligence and Security Command'.

22. Taped telephone conversation with Dr Scott Jones, 17 August 1992.

23. Taped telephone conversation with Maj. Edward Dames, 27 June 1992; and The Bulletin of Atomic Scientists, December 1992, p. 6.

24. 'The Warrior's Edge', Col. John B. Alexander, Maj. Richard Groller and Janet Morris, (William Morrow Inc., New York, 1990).

25. Ibid. p. 9.

26. Ibid. pp. 9 and 10.

27. Ibid. p. 47.

28. Ibid.

29. Ibid.

30. Ibid. pp. 72 – 3.

31. Ibid. p.12.

32. Ibid. p.13.

33. Taped telephone conversation with Janet Morris, 1 March 1993.

34 In 1989 a US Department of Defense consultant and contractor explained to the author how he was guven the task of examining the possibility of devising operational methods of transmitting subliminal messages through the TV screen.

35. 'Will the Real Scott Jones please stand up' – unpublished paper by George Hansen and Robert Durant, 20 February 1990, pp. 4 and 5.

36. 'The Birds', Armen Victorian, in UK UFO Magazine, Vol. 11 No. 3, July/August 1992, pp 4-7.

37. Out There, Howard Blum (Simon and Schuster, London 1990) pp. 44, 46-51, 55-57.

38. DIA's letters to author dated 12 July 1991, 8 July 1992 and 18 December 1992.

39. Dr Christopher 'Kit' Green, BLUEJAY, has admitted that the CIA has compiled over 30,000 files on UFOs, 200 of which are extremely interesting. Green was a key CIA member in examining the UFO problem for several years.

40. Los Alamos National Laboratory, Institutional Plan Fiscal Year 1992 – Fiscal Year 1997, p. 14.

Chapter Fifteen

Waging War

'Isn't it true that when those poor devils
stop suffering it is through a loss of
what you call psyche?.'[1]

The former Soviet Union had a long history of psychic manipulation programmes using techniques such as energetics, psycho-energetics technology or psychotronics – the use of radiated energy. The initial work on the science underpinning this area had been done in the West and was subsequently smuggled to the Soviet Union. For decades the scientific community of the West ignored the work of people like Moray Abrams, Hieronymous, Tesla, De la Warr, Down and Reich, so giving the Soviets at least a 30 years head start to build and consolidate their position in psychotronic weaponry. At the 1978 SALT peace talks, the Russian President Leonid Brezhnev suggested banning weapons 'more frightful than the mind of man has ever conceived.' But President Carter, ignorant of the advances the Soviets had made, had no idea what he was alluding to.

Some sections of the US government had, however, woken up to the reality of psychotronics. As already touched on, from 1960 to 1965 the American Embassy in Moscow was targeted by a mixture of electromagnetic and microwaves causing a wide range of physical and mental illness among US personnel serving there, which culminated in the eventual death of the US Ambassador. Dr Stephen Possony, one time Science Advisor to the Department of Defense, now retired, said to me: 'After the death of our Ambassador in Moscow, due to contracting leukaemia, and a couple of other employees, it suddenly dawned on us to have a real careful look at what was happening there.'

The Mind Controllers

Project PANDORA was initiated as a consequence, and it included a number of parallel projects with names such as TUMS, MUTS, and BAZAR. They involved the CIA, Advanced Research Project Agency (ARPA), the State Department, the Navy and the Army who were 'tasked' to study the effects of the emitted Soviet microwaves on animals and humans.

The extent of the US's worries can be gauged by a confidential telegram sent by the US Ambassador in Moscow, signed by Brement, to the Secretary of State in Washington DC, in April 1976: '... Another adverse factor is the exposure of employees and dependents to significant levels of electromagnetic radiation which is aimed at the embassy complex by Soviet sources. The situation has greatly increased the emotional stress and worry of employees and their families. This problem is particularly acute for the thirty-five employees who both live and work in the embassy and their dependents including in some cases pregnant women and children. Whatever the physical and health effects of exposure to electromagnetic radiation, most employees and a significant number of families now have additional source of anxiety and worry in a population already subject to a unique variety of emotional stresses. Additional classified info on this topic is available in A/SY and M/MED.

'... During the last few weeks Soviet authorities have undertaken a vigorous and intensive campaign of harassment against embassy employees and their families. During the course of a recent night more than 70 telephone calls were received by various employees and their families. In addition to making it difficult to sleep, these calls often threaten, violences against the employees and his family. On occassion specific threats were made against children. A number of officers have received death threats; others have been subject to involuntary detention and jostling by gang of Soviet nationals. Further examples of threats include; playing funeral music on the telephone to an employee's youngster, damage to privately owned vehicles and repeated bomb threats which have required the evacuation of the embassy and chancery living quarters.'

The electromagnetic waves beamed at the embassy, which were subsequently named the 'Moscow Signals', were in the short 'S' and long 'L' spectrum and had complex modulations, some of which were random. A 'Top Secret-Eyes Only' memorandum, dated 20 December 1966 from ARPA shows the significance of this threat:

'The White House has directed, through USIB [US Intelligence Board] that intensive investigative research be conducted within the State Department, CIA and DoD to attempt to determine what the threat is. The national programme has been co-ordinated by the State Department, under the code name 'TUMS'. ARPA is represented and is conducting research on a selective portion of the overall programme concerned with one of the potential threats, that of the effects of low level electromagnetic radiation on man. This memorandum summarises the initial results obtained from this programme called Pandora.'

In April 1976 the Secretary of State Henry Kissinger sent the following telegram to the US Embassy in Moscow which summarised the conclusions of studies of the Moscow signal.

'Subject: Radiation and UHF and Electromagnetic Dangers:

'1. On April 6 AFSA president John Hemenway submitted the following report to AFSA's governing board:

'2. Begin text: 'Beginning in 1960 the Soviet Union directed the high frequency beams of radiation at the US Embassy in Moscow which were calculated not to pick up intelligence but cause physiological effects on personnel.

'The effects the Soviets calculated to achieve in the personnel serving (at least as early as 1960) included

The Mind Controllers

(A) Malaise (B) Irritability, (C) Extreme fatigue. At this time the Soviets believed that the induced effects were temporary.

'Subsequently, it has been verified that the effects are not temporary. Definitely tied to such radiation and the UHF/VHF electromagnetic waves are: (A) Cataracts, (B) Blood changes that induce heart attacks, (C) Malignancies, (D) Circulatory problems, and (E) Permanent deterioration of the nervous system.

'In most cases the after-effects do not become evident until long after exposure – a decade or more.'

The Soviet's research was clearly worrying the US, although of course no public admission of this was made. And there was good reason to be concerned; for example, in 1974, V.P. Kaznacheyev believed that he had demonstrated death could be caused by beaming ultraviolet rays from a distance.[2] In the same year, Robert Pavlita, a Czech engineer, showed how he could kill insects at a distance by using psychotronic devices.

It has been reported by US intelligence that Pavlita developed two psychotronic weapons – one effective at 320 kilometres, and the other effective at any distance, capable of inducing powerful and uncontrollable emotions, seizure, paralysis or death. At that time, Pavlita had thirty years experience of building psychotronic generators.[3]

Anecdotal evidence of similar work continued to emerge in the West. An American biophysicist who participated in an exchange programme at the University of Prague in 1979 told me: 'Just prior to my arrival an East German graduate student was killed there while working on a project using a superconducting waveguide [a cryogenically cooled device that aligns and aims radio waves with great precision]. What is surprising is what happened next. The Soviets had the entire wall of the physics lab ripped out and all the cryo-equipment, wave guides, and other gear shipped to a castle near the Czech-USSR border.'

The biophysicist went on, 'I learned from other professors who helped with the project that after a few months Soviet scientists were able to kill goats at ranges beyond one kilometre and to cause disorientating or incapacitating effects depending on the aspect angle of the goats' heads at well over two kilometres.'[4]

After the 'Moscow signals', the next Soviet activity which caused alarm in the United States was the so-called 'Woodpecker signals', which were first detected in late 1975 and continued for some time after. These high frequency signals which could be picked up on domestic radios at 21 MHz, had a repetitive sound like 'tock, tock, tock' – hence the name 'Woodpecker'.[5]

Their source was eventually tracked down to three stations in Riga, Latvia. Each emitted signal was 25-30 times stronger than the earth's natural background electromagnetic field, which has a frequency of 7-7.5 Hz. Those analysing the signals came up with the theory that the brains of mammals are naturally tuned into the 7-7.5 Hz frequency but 25% would be affected by 10 Hz Woodpecker signals. In turn it was thought that these modulations could be adapted to carry any type of message which could be pumped directly into the brain.

The frequent changes in the characteristics of the transmitted pulse, as well as the frequency of the transmission, suggested the signal was used for remote control or telemetry. However, based on intelligence gathered by the Defense Intelligence Agency, it was decided the Woodpecker transmissions were in fact the Soviet Union's first attempt to develop over-the-horizon-radar (OTHR).

The first radar site was constructed in 1975 and tests were conducted for several years. It turned out that the electromagnetic signal was being attenuated while passing through the Polar Ionosphere. Of ten missiles launched, the radar could only guarantee detection of some.[6] 'Woodpecker' was the brainchild of F. Kuzminskiy, the chief designer, who later became the Director of NII (Scientific Research Institute). An internal power struggle between Kuzminskiy and Vladimir Ivanovich Markov, a Technical Science Advisor, brought the project to a halt. Despite apparently solving the system's problems, Kuzminskiy was unable to obtain the backing of the Soviet regime and it was never completed.[7]

The DIA report on the 'Woodpecker' system makes repeated reference to Kuzminskiy's work as a 'weapons system', but it is now clear it was not deliberately designed to tamper with the brain. Yet upon its discovery by the US it was believed to be for that purpose, possibly a means for 'controlling the world's weather, creating physiological or psychological effects on people outside the USSR.'[8]

Similar attributes are now being applied to the US Department of Defense's HAARP programme, under construction in Alaska, USA.[9] Trying to play catch-up, the US Army and Navy embarked on intensive research programmes encompassing aspects of electromagnetics, microwaves, radio transmissions and so on. Most of these programmes were, and remain, highly classified.

Some sections which had not been initially classified were reclassified in the late 1970s. Wherever and whenever there were areas of interest in these programmes, the CIA stepped in and, by funding them, extended the research dimension, and shared the results. Laws were introduced to curtail any inquiries made by the public, and university authorities were banned from questioning the members of their own academic fraternity engaged in such programmes.

Educational values and ethics became irrelevant. A similar situation pertains on the campuses of some British universities.[10] The results of some of the experimental programmes were shocking.[11]

Various military and intelligence establishments had suspicions about the possible harmful effects of non-ionising electromagnetic radiation and microwaves on humans. The Defense Intelligence Agency, the CIA and the Army had been monitoring the progress made by the Soviet Union and its satellites for decades. Despite the intelligence reports on the harmful effects of Electromagnetic Radiation (EMR) and microwaves, they decided to try to establish the facts themselves. The Pandora programme was in effect a stepping-stone. Extensive testing was conducted in the Army, Navy, Air Force and CIA, either through contractors or in their own laboratories.

Contractors provided them with non-volunteer human testers. Several military contracts involved working in highly dangerous environments. Some still do. At times, their employers were aware of this, and yet allowed it to continue. There were two main reasons: (a) to comply with the terms of the lucrative contracts; (b) to gather data about the effects of irradiation on humans.

Years later a flood of court cases brought by unwitting victims once more raised the serious question: does the end justify the means? After all, those responsible in several cases were indeed aware of the harmful effects of EMR, and yet they had deliberately concealed the facts from their victims or employees. Several lives were lost, yet no liability has ever been admitted by the establishments or their contractors. The situation remains the same today.[12]

US military interest in electromagnetics is now well established. The Tri-Service Electromagnetic Advisory Panel (TERP) represents the interests of all three military services in the US. When the TERP was established, the Memorandum of Understanding, dated 21 July 1980, was signed by military representatives including: Major General John W. Ord, USAF, MC, Commander, Aerospace Medical Division of Air Force Systems Command; Brigadier General Garrison Rapmund, MC, Commander, US Army Medical Research and Development Command; and Captain John D. Bloom, MC, USN, Commanding Officer, Naval

Medical Research and Development Command.

A further Memorandum of Understanding of 1990 states that:

'PURPOSE: This Tri-Service Panel is re-established and re-chartered to ensure a visible, effective co-ordination of efforts by the military departments, each possessing common and service unique requirements to conduct research and development on the biological effects of non-ionising Electromagentic Radiation (EMR) on man.

'OBJECTIVE: a. Identify and periodically review those medical research and developments regarding biological effects of non-ionising EMR which are common to the three military departments and those requirements which are mission specific to a single department.

'b. Identify medical research and development objectives which are responsible to the needs of the military operating forces, systems developers, and the military scientific and technical community.

'c. Coordinate utilisation of facilities, material, personnel and funds to accomplish the required research and development in a timely and effective manner.

'd. Develop procedures for continuing interservice exchange of information on all aspects of ongoing research and development on the effects of non-ionising EMR on man.

'e. Develop procedures for the coordination of research and development in this area by the three military departments with other agencies.'

The membership of TERP consists of three full-time military or civilian employees who are selected by the Army, Navy, the Air Force and the Marine Corps. The panel regularly calls in distinguished members of the scientific community for further advice and progress. It serves as an advisory body to the Office of the Secretary of Defense (OSD) and other offices within the Office of the Assistant Secretary of Defense (OASD) but it does not limit its research to within the military and has an active interest in national research.

TERP's research covered a wide area in 1990. For example, the Army's interest in the biological effects of non-nuclear electromagentic pulses led to study and research in areas such as human dosimetry and 'bio-effects' of high peak pulsed electromagnetic fields, and the development of an occupational and environmental non-nuclear electromagnetic injury data base.

It was regarded as vital to learn the effects such fields have on humans. A number of civilians were the target of covert experiments in this field, both in Europe and the US, but they have failed to identify who was responsible for their mistreatment. Their efforts to obtain support from their politicians or from various international victim support organisations, such as Amnesty International and the Medical Foundation for the Care of Victims of Torture have produced no results.[13] The US Air Force has also been conducting research into eye injury caused by exposure to millimetre wave systems, and the biological effects of 'high power microwave in low microwave regions (S band).' The minutes of a TERP meeting held at the USAF School of Aerospace Medicine, in Brooks Air Force Base, Texas, on 27/28 October 1987, began: 'The Radio Frequency Radiation (RFR) behavioral programme at Walter Reed Army Institute of Research (WRAIR) is considered high priority.'

The use of High Power Microwave (HMP), developed at Los Alamos, Lawrence Livermore or Sandia laboratories, by each of the military services seems to be commonplace. A letter dated 18 March 1986, concerning the TERP meeting of 10-13 February 1986 noted that, 'The Army will take deliver of a 2.5 GHz system developed by Sandia on 3 March 1986.' The same letter noted that 'The biological studies will emphasize the eye, heart and behaviour.'

The Department of Defense keeps track of medical research in this field. Minutes from TERP's meeting on

The Mind Controllers

1 May 1989 recommends that 'any medical surveillance criteria' on the 'vulnerability, survivability and effects of Electro-magnetic Beams' would play a crucial role in the outcome of research.[14]

The US Navy seems the most interested. The list of programmes released by the Office of the Chief of Naval Research (OCNR)[15] on the biological effects of electromagnetic waves is monumental. The index alone in April 1989 came to five volumes, providing a brief glimpse into each programme, and this surely gives an indication into the extent of research.[16] The programmes vary from the use of body current to assess absorption rates of Very Low Frequency (VLF) and High Frequency (HF) transmissions, biological effects of magnetic fields, the development of effective electromagnetic field surveillance, and the effects of EM on genes and DNA – to topics akin to science fiction, such as electroportation (synthetic teleportation).[17] The scope and results of these studies, while scientifically invaluable, could have far-reaching and frightening implications if they are further modified to be used offensively.

By taking advantage of the Electromagnetic (EMF) technology, it appears that various intelligence agencies have developed considerable capabilities. The NSA has shown great interest in developing the potential of technology to remotely monitor the EEG (brain waves) of subjects. Should such technology be developed, and the EEG of the targeted individual decoded, it would enable the agency not only to study the thought processes of the targeted individual, but it might be able to influence the thinking patterns of the decision-making processes of such targets.

Already preliminary progress has been made. Dr Donald York, a neurophysiologist, and Dr Thomas Jensen, a speech pathologist, from the University of Missouri, have been able to identify and decode 27 words and syllables in specific brain wave patterns. They have been able to correlate these EEG patterns with both spoken words and the silent thought words in 40 subjects. They produced a computer programme with the brain wave vocabulary. The aim was to help stroke victims who have lost their speech powers.[18]

At the height of the Remote Viewing programmes, several intelligence organisations in the US, such as the CIA, the Army and the DIA, embarked on intensive study of the EEG of their remote viewers. The idea was to try to ascertain how information is obtained by the viewers, and whether, by reversing the process, information given to the viewer could be passed on to influence the target. Los Alamos National Laboratory (LANL) conducted extensive research programmes in this area.

The US Air Force reported in 1996: 'Modern electromagnetic scattering theory raises the prospect that ultrashort pulse scattering through the human brain can result in reflected signals that can be used to construct a reliable estimate of the degree of central nervous system arousal. The concept behind this "remote EEG" is to scatter off of action potentials or ensembles of action potentials in major nervous system tracts. Assuming we will understand how our skills are imprinted and recalled, it might be possible to take this concept one step further and duplicate the experience set in another individual. The prospect of providing a "been there-done that" knowledge-base could provide a revolutionary change in our approach to specialised training. The impact of success would boggle the mind.'[19]

In recent years a number of mind control programmes have embraced the non-lethal weapons concept. One example is infrasound weapons that incorporate a Very Low Frequency (VLF) or Radio Frequency (RF) modulation to cause nausea, abdominal spasm and vomiting. A confidential report prepared by the US Army Mobility Equipment Research and Development Center, Fort Believer, Virginia, as early as 1969 detailed the effect an infrasonic system would have on humans. These effects range from disruption of nervous systems to death.[20] Records show that Los Alamos National Laboratory in 1994 conducted a research and development programme with the support of the US Army Research, Development and Engineering Center (ARDEC) on the design and performance of microwave weapons.[21] Some of these weapons might have been previously used by US agencies and departments covertly in the US and UK.

Furthermore, in a recent letter from the US Department of Defense (in response to one of my Freedom of Information Act requests, pending since 1994) for acoustic generators (anti-personnel, anti-material) high-power microwave generators, neural inhibitors, and wireless stun technology, I was informed that the information I sought is now in the purview of the previously unknown Non-Lethal Weapons Directorate.[22]

A classified conference was organised by the Los Alamos National Laboratory, with the support of the American Defense Preparedness Association on 16/17 November 1993. The following speakers presented papers on various topics relating to mind control, as part of the new, non-lethal weapons concept: Dr George Baker (Defense Nuclear Agency – now Defense Special Weapons Agency, DSWA): 'Radio Frequency Weapons – a very attractive non-lethal option'; Dr John Derring (Scientific Applications Research Associate – SARA): 'Acoustic Technology'; Dr Clay Easterly (Oak Ridge National Laboratory): 'Application of ELF Fields to non-lethal weapons'; Ms Astrid Lewis (US Army Chemical Research and Development Command): 'Chemical/Biological Anti-Terrorism'.

The United Kingdom, too, has played a role in the study of microwaves for defence applications. Professor E.H. Grant and Dr R. J. Sheppard from Queen Elizabeth College have been working in this field. Grant has carried out an enormous amount of work commissioned by the US Air Force, as has Sheppard for the Navy. Grant has delivered several lectures as the principal scientist at the NATO Advanced Research Group.[23] During 1983-4 Sheppard was working with the US Air Force, Torry Research Station and GEC Ltd.[24]

My inquiries directed towards GCHQ about their current programmes concerning the use of pulsed microwaves for defence use were only answered by the Foreign and Commonwealth Office after a long delay. They informed me that such programmes have been granted to various universities, and that GCHQ does not conduct any independent research into these matters.[25]

That such weapons have been used can be in little doubt. When the deployment of Cruise missiles at American bases in the UK was at its height, women peace campaigners staged a series of highly publicised peaceful protests outside the perimeter wires. In late 1985 the women living in the peace camps at Greenham Common began to experience unusual patterns of illness, ranging from severe headaches, drowsiness, menstrual bleeding at abnormal times, or after the onset of menopause, to bouts of temporary paralysis and faulty speech co-ordination. There were also reports of two spontaneous abortions occurring five months into the pregnancy, which is considered to be unusually late. Suspicious of the possible use of electromagnetic biological weapons, the women looked for help. 'Electronics Today' magazine carried out a number of measurements and in December 1985 published their report which concluded: 'Readings taken with a wide range of signal strength meters showed marked increases in the background signal level near one of the women's camps at a time when they claimed to be experiencing ill effects.' They noted that if the women created noise or a disturbance near the fence, the signals rose sharply.

In 'Peace Women fear electronic zapping at base' in The Guardian, 10 March 1986, Gareth Parry reported that, 'The American military [at Greenham Common] have an intruder detection system called BISS, Base Installation Security System, which operates on a sufficiently high frequency to bounce radar waves off a human body moving in the vicinity of a perimeter fence.' In a hearing before a Subcommittee of the Committee on Appropriations, US House of Representatives, on Military Construction Appropriations for 1985, General Schneidel made an indiscreet reference to the possibility of the use of microwave weapons at Greenham Common.

Speaking in a form of military gobbledegook he said: 'The concept of our operations is to protect the highest value resources on the base. We have a set concept that provides for security while in garrison and certainly in wartime, when it deploys off the installation and into the operational mode. Whatever the case may be, where the system is not full up with all the required sensors, fences and lights, people will be assigned to compensate for those shortfalls in the equipment.'

After the deployment of the microwave security system, the number of US personnel guarding the installation fell dramatically. The deployment of this security measure was further indirectly confirmed through the year-end report of the Department of the Air Force Headquarters 501st, Security Police Group: 'The Greenham Common by-laws went into effect, the superfence was constructed .'[26]

It is not clear whether the Greenham women were targeted by a microwave weapon or were irradiated by prolonged proximity to a microwave security fence. But since the US authorities at Greenham did not alert the protesters to the dangers of such a fence, it comes to much the same thing.[27] The effects of non-ionising radiation on humans was well-known to the US authorities.[28]

The late Kim Besly, a veteran peace campaigner and frequent visitor to Greenham Common, in the conclusion of her report on the irradiation of the Greenham women, written on 30 October 1986, asked, 'Do we have to wait three generations for "hard evidence"?'[29] Liz Westmoreland from Peace and Emergency told me recently that several women peace campaigners from Greenham Common are suffering from various types of cancer. Is it possible that the US made use of lessons learned from a Cold War adversary to harm and intimidate the citizens of one of her closest allies? The full facts have yet to be unearthed.

Many possible victims of mind control, claiming to hear voices in their heads, are dismissed as needing psychiatric help. But the evidence in hand suggests that the technology to produce 'voices in the head' does exist. For many years the technology of altering and/or influencing the human mind with the help of new electronic technology, has been the subject of several projects and programmes by military and intelligence organisations in the west, especially the US. Here are some examples.

A US Patent reveals details of a Psycho-Acoustic Projector: 'Broadly this disclosure is directed to a system for producing aural psychological disturbances and partial deafness of the enemy during combat situations. Essentially, a high directional beam is radiated from a plurality of distinct transducers and is modulated by a noise, code or speech beat signal. The invention may utilise various forms and may include movable radiators mounted on a vehicle, or means employed to modulate the acoustical beam with respect to a fixed frequency.'[30] The purpose of this weapon is clearly to provide intense aural and psychological disturbance in the target, thereby immobilising him or her.

Another patent discusses methods and system for altering consciousness. The Department of Defense had already acquired the technology to alter consciousness through various projects and programmes. The abstract from one such programme states: 'A system for altering the states of human consciousness involves the simultaneous application of multiple stimuli, preferably sounds, having different frequencies and wave forms.'[31] From another: 'Researchers have devised a variety of systems for stimulating the brain to exhibit specific brain wave rhythms and thereby alter the state of consciousness of the individual subject.'[32]

Silent subliminal messages are also a fertile area of activity. Dr Oliver M. Lowry has participated in several classified projects for the US Government on what is termed in the military and intelligence world as Silent Sound Spread Spectrum (SSSS), sometimes also known as SQUAD. The President of Silent Sound Incorporation, Edward Tilton, wrote to me saying that 'The system was used throughout Operation Desert Storm (Iraq) quite successfully.'[33] Lowry provides a glimpse into the use of such technology: 'A silent communications system in which non-aural carriers, in the very low or very high audio frequency range or in the adjacent ultrasonic frequency spectrum, are amplified or frequency modulated with the desired intelligence and propagated acoustically or vibrationally, for inducement into the brain. The modulated carriers may be transmitted directly in real time or may be conveniently recorded and stored on mechanical, magnetic or optical media for delayed or repeated transmission to the listener.'[34]

Various types of apparatus and modes of application have been tested and used to 'inject' intelligible sounds into the heads of human beings. Sound could also be induced in someone's head by radiating the head with radio wavers including microwaves in the range of 100 to 10,000 Mhz, that are modulated with a particular waveform. The waveform consists of frequency modulated bursts. Each burst is made up of ten to twenty uniformly spaced pulses grouped tightly together. The burst width is between 500 nanoseconds and 100 microseconds. The pulse width is in the range of 10 nanoseconds to one microsecond. The bursts are frequently modulated by the audio input to create the sensation of hearing in the person whose head is irradiated.

The latest development in the technology of induced fear and mind control is, in effect, the cloning of the human EEG or brain waves of any targeted victim, or indeed groups. With the use of powerful computers, segments of human emotions which include anger, anguish, anxiety, contempt, despair, dread, embarrassment, envy, fear, frustration, grief, guilt, hate, indifference, indignation, jealousy, pity, rage, regret, remorse, resentment, sadness, shame, spite and terror have been identified and isolated within the EEG signals as 'emotion signature clusters'. Their relevant frequencies and amplitudes have been measured, then the very frequency/amplitude cluster is synthesised and stored on another computer, each one of these negative emotions properly and separately tagged. They are then placed on the Silent Sound carrier frequencies and could silently trigger the occurrence of the same basic emotion in another human being.

Footnotes:

1. Dr Walter Freeman, the first person to practice frontal lobe lobotomy to alter minds. He conducted over 3,500 lobotomies. Lobotomy is still very much in use to today, in Scotland and Sweden in particular.

2. V.P. Kaznacheyev et al, 'Apparent Information Transfer Between Two Groups of Cells', Psychoenergetic System, Vol. 1, December 1974, and 'Distant Intercellular Interactions in a System of Two Issue Cultures', Psychoenergetic System, Vol. 1 no. 3, March 1976. John Alexander, the founding father of the non-lethal weapon concept, also has a keen interest in this subject. Several of his on the record conversations with various American researchers, examining the possibilities of inducing illness from a distance, are in my archives.

3. Defense Intelligence Agency Report DST-180S-387-75, 'Soviet and Czechoslovakian Parapsychology Research,' 1988. 4. The Atlantic , Vol. 259, March 1987 p. 24. 5. The 'Woodpecker' signals started operating at the start of the eleven year solar cycle, when sunspot activities, which interfere with commercial radio systems, are at their peak. Whether it was an attempt by the Soviets to hide the 'Woodpecker' in the solar activity, or the solar activity increased the effects of Woodpecker, is unknown.

6. Defense Intelligence Agency JPRS Report, Soviet Union; Military Affairs, 3 May 1991.

7. DIA Report (note 5).

8. F.C. Judd, 'The Russian Woodpecker: Has it become an extinct species?' in Short Wave Magazine March 1991.

9. Oddly enough, the Lawrence Livermore National Laboratories (LLNL) also has a highly classified programme called 'Woodpecker', though LLNL's programme seems more in tune with their efforts in the development of non-lethal weapons, some affecting the human mind. Various correspondence with Lawrence Livermore.

10. For more details on the activities of the British military in universities, see The Campus Connection – Military Research on Campus by Rob Evans, Nicola Butler and Eddie Gonsalves, Student CND, London 1991.

11. The Naval Aerospace Medical Research Laboratory in Pensacola, Florida, in the course of their tests carried out in Project SANGUINE, in Clam Lake, discovered that exposure to the magnetic field component in the SANGUINE antenna – within an ELF field of 45 to 74 Hz. – produced stress identical to that induced by gross alcohol consumption: Records released by the US Navy on Project SANGUINE to the author. See also Robert Becker, Cross Currents, Jeremy P. Tarcher Inc., Los Angeles, USA, 1990, p. 202.

12. See my 'The Killing of Robert Strom', in Open Eye no. 3, 1995. The Strom story was covered by CBS News' 'Sixty Minutes', 'Strom vs. Boeing', produced by David Aummel, 5 March 1989.

13. e.g. The Verneys. I have corresponded with the Home Office,

Amnesty International and the Medical Foundation for the Care of Victims of Torture without positive results. My archives contain several files from individuals of high intellect, who say they have been, and in some cases still are, subjected to daily torture by electromagnetic means. To date no organisation has admitted responsibility for this, nor has their plight been listened to by any victim support organization.

14. Meeting Report of TERP, 1 May 1989, p. 2.

15. Letter to author from Lois Welch, Office of the Chief of Naval Research, 13 February 1991.

16. Biological Effects of Nonionizing Electromagnetic Radiation, Vol. XII, numbers 1 to 5, December 1988; Office of the Chief of Naval Research, Arlington, Virginia, published April 1989.

17. Example of one sci-fi type project is Project Code 441k708-04. 'Electroportation: Theory of Basic Mechanisms – Progress: the quantitive theory successfully describes reversible electrical breakdown of a bilayer membrane due to large electrical pulse and passive charging with the retention of the charge due to small pulse.'

'The scientists at Lawrence Livermore National Laboratories, a centre of nuclear research, talk about such things as brain bombs – being able to take energy of a nuclear weapon and focus it into a selection portion of the lower end of the electro-magnetic spectrum, and being able to use that energy to affect the enemy's brain. The idea would be to have enemy soldiers drop in their tracks.' The Atlantic Vol. 259 March 1987.

18. Personal correspondence with the author, 1994.

19. 'Biological Process Control', in New World Vistas – Air and Space Power for the Twenty-first Century, US Air Force, 1996, p. 90

20. 'An Infrasonic System', US Army Mobility Equipment Research and Development Center, Fort Believer, VA, 1969. See section on 'Effects-Human'. In a forthcoming book, 'The Future War', John Alexander, one of the supporters, forerunners and founding fathers of the non-lethal weapons concept, tries to legitimize the acquisition and deployment of these destructive

weapons.

21. LA-CP-94-0061, Microwave Weapon Design and Performance Envelope, work supported by the US Army Research, Development and Engineering Center (ARDEC), Picatinny Arsenal, New Jersey.LA-UR-83-150, 'Microwave Related Efforts at the Los Alamos National Laboratory', submitted to: High Power Microwave Technology Conference, Harry Diamond Laboratory, Aldephi, Maryland, 1-3 March, 1983.

22. Letter of 2 October 1997 from William A. Longwell, Acting Counsel, Marine Systems Command to author, concerning a request filed in 1994. See also 'Pentagon to set priorities in non-lethal Technologies' in Inside the Air Force: an exclusive weekly report on Air Force programmes, procurement and policy-making, Vol. 5 no. 15 April 1994.

23. Grant was the principal scientific witness for Mercury Communications Ltd. in their successful appeal under the 1971 Town and Country Planning Act against the refusal by Manchester City Council to allow the installation of a microwave tower on the grounds that it would be a health hazard.

24. Queen Elizabeth College Annual Report, 1983-4, p. 31.

25. Letter from FCO to author, 1993.

26. APO New York 09150, 5 December 1985.

27. Eldon Byrd, a scientist for the Naval Surface Weapon Centre, USN, in one of his lectures in 1986 on the effects of microwaves stated: 'We can alter the behaviour of tissues, cells, organs and whole organisms you can cause up to six times higher foetus mortality and birth defects in laboratory animals, and these fields are so weak you can hardly detect them You can do genetic engineering with ELF [extremely low frequency] weak magnetic fields without micro-surgical techniques that are currently employed to do genetic engineering. It is known how to induce malignant diseases in human cells and how to cure them. You can entrain human beings' brain waves across a room with a very weak magnetic field.' Taped lectures in author's possession.

28. Preliminary Report – Background information Microwave/Electromagnetic Pollution: a little known hazard,

October 1986, updated June 1988.

29. Besly died of cancer in 1996.

30. Psycho-Acoustic Projector, Patent 3,566,347, US Patent Office, 23 February 1971.

31. Method and System for Altering Consciousness, Patent 5,289,438, US Patent Office 22 February 1994.

32. Method and System for Altering Consciousness, Patent 5,123,899, dated 23 June 1992.

33. Letter from Edward Tilton 13 December 1996.

34. Silent Subliminal Presentation, Patent 5,159,703, US Patent Office, 27 October 1992.

Index

Index

Index

Index

Index

Index